6 -
scan

LONDON, NEW YORK, MUNICH,
MELBOURNE, AND DELHI

Editor **Michael Slind**
Project Art Editor **Jason Godfrey at Godfrey Design**
Senior Editor **Dawn Henderson**
DTP Design and Reproduction **Adam Walker**
Production Controller **Luca Frassinetti**
Managing Editor **Julie Oughton**
Managing Art Editor **Heather McCarry**
Publishing Manager **Adèle Hayward**
Category Publisher **Stephanie Jackson**
Art Director **Peter Luff**

First published in the USA in 2005 by
DK Publishing, Inc.
375 Hudson Street, New York, NY 10014

First published in Great Britain in 2005 by
Dorling Kindersley Limited,
80 Strand, London WC2R 0RL
A Penguin Company

2 4 6 8 10 9 7 5 3 1

DK books are available at special discounts for bulk purchases for sales promotions,
premiums, fund-raising, or educational use. For details contact: SpecialSales@dk.com

A Cataloging-in-Publication record for this book
is available from the Library of Congress.
(US) ISBN 0-7566-1057-5

A CIP catalog record for this book
is available from the British Library.
(UK) ISBN 1 4053 0259 3

Reproduced by Colourscan, Singapore
Printed and bound in Italy by Graphicom

Discover more at
www.dk.com

CONTENTS

INTRODUCTION

Re-imagining … What's Essential

Fall 2003. I publish my Big Book … *Business Excellence in a Disruptive Age*. It is, since the publication of *In Search of Excellen*ce in 1982, my most ambitious attempt to state comprehensively … What Business Is. (Or Could Be.) (Or *Must* Be.)

The year following, 2004. While traveling to promote the book … and while keeping up with my usual speaking and consulting schedule… I note a steadily increasing drumbeat. A drumbeat of consternation around the issue of "outsourcing." (Or "off-shoring.") Jobs going to India. Or China. Or just … Somewhere Else.

What is to be done? How can people cope … with the specter of … massive job shrinkage? My (nutshell) answer: Job shrinkage is inevitable. Whether because of outsourcing or automation (which, long-term, may be a bigger deal than outsourcing), you can't count on any job being "there for you." What you can do is find ways to move yourself and your company Up the Value Chain … and into the heart and soul of the New Economy.

Summer 2005. I publish a series of four quick and to-the-point books, one of which you now hold in your hand. The "Essentials" is what the series is called. As in: Here are the essential things you *must* know … as you strive to *act* … in this unstable, up-tempo, outsourcing-addled, out-of-this-world age.

New Economy, New Mandate, New Story

A lot of yogurt has hit the fan. In the near term, globalization continues to be a mixed blessing—a worthy end point, but messy and uneven to the extreme in its immediate impact. Waves of technological change engulf us—and confuse us. Corporate scandals erupt. Once-mighty titans (namely: big companies and the CEOs who lead them) fall from their lofty perches

And yet ... there *is* a New Economy.

Would you change places with your grandfather? Would you want to work 11 brutal hours a day ... in yesterday's Bethlehem Steel mill, or a Ford Motor Company factory circa 1935? Not me. Nor would I change places with my father ... who labored in a white-collar sweatshop, at the same company, in the same building, for 41 l-o-n-g years.

A workplace revolution is under way. No sensible person expects to spend a lifetime in a single corporation anymore. Some call this shift the "end of corporate responsibility." I call it ... the Beginning of Renewed Individual Responsibility. An extraordinary opportunity to take charge of our own lives.

Put me in charge! Make me Chairman and CEO and President and COO of Tom Inc.

That's what I ask! (Beg, in fact.)

I *love* business at its best. When it aims to foster growth and deliver exciting services to its clients and exciting opportunities to its employees. I especially *love* business at this moment of flux. This truly magical, albeit in many ways terrifying, moment.

I'm no Pollyanna. I've been around. (And then around.) My rose-colored glasses were long ago ground to powder by brutal reality.

Yet I am hopeful. Not hopeful that human beings will become more benign ... or that evil will evaporate ... or that greed will be regulated out of existence. But I am hopeful that in the New Economy people will see the power that comes from taking responsibility for their professional lives. And I am hopeful that they also will find pleasure in unleashing their instinctive curiosity and creativity.

The harsh news: This is Not Optional. The microchip will colonize all rote activities. And we will have to scramble to reinvent ourselves—as we did when we came off the farm and went into the factory, and then as we were ejected from the factory and delivered to the white-collar towers.

The exciting news (as I see it, anyway): This is Not Optional. The reinvented *you* and the reinvented *me* will have no choice but to scramble and add value in some meaningful way.

The Back-Story: A Tale/Trail of Disruption

Each book in the series builds on a central premise—the same premise that I propounded in the early chapters of *Re-imagine*! Herewith, an Executive Summary of that Progression of Ideas.

1. All bets are off. It is the foremost task—and responsibility—of our generation to re-imagine our enterprises and institutions, public and private. Rather strong rhetoric. But I believe it. The fundamental nature of the change now in progress has caught us off-stride and on our heels. No aspect of the way our institutions operate can be allowed to go unexamined. Or unchanged.

2. We are in a ... Brawl with No Rules. Business, politics, and, indeed, the essential nature of human interchange have come unglued. We have to make things up as we go along. (Success = SAV = "Screw Around Vigorously.") ("Fail. Forward. Fast.") Yesterday's strictures and structures leave us laughably—and tragically—unprepared for this Brawl with No Rules. From al Qaeda to Wal*Mart, new entrants on the world stage have flummoxed regnant institutions and their leaders.

3. Incrementalism is *Out*. Destruction is *In*. "Continuous improvement," the lead mantra of 1980s management, is now downright dangerous. All or nothing. ("Control. Alt. Delete.") We must gut the innards of our enterprises before new competitors do it for us—and to us.

4. InfoTech changes everything. There is no higher priority than the Total Transformation of all business practice to e-business practice. The new technologies are ... The Real Thing. The IT Revolution is in its infancy. And yet it has already changed the rules—changed them so fundamentally that years and years will pass before we can begin talking about constructing a new rule book.

5. Ninety percent of white-collar jobs as we know them (and, ultimately, 90 percent of all jobs as we know them) will be disemboweled in the next 15 years. Done. Gone. Kaput. Between the microprocessor, 60/60/24/7 connectivity, and outsourcing to developing countries, the developed nations' white-collar jobs are ... doomed. Time frame? Zero to 15 or 20 years. How confident am I on this point? Totally.

6. "Winners" (survivors!) will become *de facto* bosses of Me Inc. Self-reliance will, of necessity, replace corporate cosseting. Old-style corporate security is evaporating. Upshot: Free the cubicle slaves! The only defense is a good offense! Hackneyed? Sure. But no less true for being so. A scary ... but also immensely exciting ... New Age of Self-Reliance is being birthed before our eyes. Hurray!

Story Time—for a Storied Time

Building on that premise, each book in this series tells a story—a saga of how we will survive (and, perhaps, go beyond survival) in this Dizzy, Disruptive Age.

A Story about *Leadership*. Command-and-control management ... "leadership" from on high ... is obsolete. New Leadership draws on a new skill set—the hallmarks of which are improvisation and inspiration. It taps into the unique leadership attributes of women. It cultivates Great Talent by creating a Great Place to Work.

A Story about *Design*. New Value-Added derives less and less from "product" or "service" quality, and more and more from ... Something More. Something called "Experiences." Something called "Branding." Something called "Design."

A Story about *Talent*. It's a Brand You World. "Lifetime employment" at a corporation (aka "cubicle slavery") is out. Lifetime self-reinvention is in. The only fool-proof source of job security is … your talent. And your talent will express itself by building a scintillating portfolio of WOW Projects and by Thinking Weird (as these weird, wild times demand).

A Story about *Trends*. Where, amid so much flux and discontinuity, are the Big Market Opportunities? They are hiding in plain sight. Go where they buyers are and where the money is—among women and among aging Boomers.

The Story Re-imagined: What's New

To tell these stories, I have adapted selected chapters from *Re-imagine!* As I've seen fit, I have nipped and tucked and otherwise revised each chapter throughout.

In addition, I—along with the folks at my publisher, Dorling Kindersley—have re-imagined the the look-and-feel of each book from the inside-out. With *Re-imagine!*, we set out to re-invent the business book. We wanted to tell the story of a world of enterprise that is bursting at the seams with revolutionary possibility, and so we created a book that bursts forth with Passion and Energy and Color. For the Essentials series, we have retained those qualities, but we have also stripped the design of these books down to its … essentials. Same Passion. Same Energy. Same Color. All in a format that fits in your hand … and meets (we believe) your essential needs.

Two new features amplify the Story Being Told.

First, capping each chapter is a list of "Top 10 To-Dos"—a one-page digest of the chapter in the form of action items that will inspire you to Do Something … right away. Here again, the emphasis is on drilling down to … what's essential.

Second, between certain chapters we include highlights from interviews with "Cool Friends"—smart people whose work has helped make me smarter. Full-text versions of these and other interviews appear on my Web site (www.tompeters.com).

Meet My PrimeTime Co-Author

For this book on what I call TrendsWorthTrillions, I call on the assistance of Martha Barletta—friend, colleague, expert on all things relating to ... Marketing to Women. In fact, *Marketing to Women* is the title of her first book. I've asked Marti to supplement my top-line "take" on that subject with her own deep-going analysis of how companies can (and *must*) reach that market. Plus, Marti's next book will be about ... PrimeTime Women. That's her term for the segment that lies at the intersection of the two big trends covered in this book: the roaring Women's Market and Maturity Mania. So, for the last chapter here, she offers a preview of that ... Convergence of Opportunity.

Last Words ...

The moral of my story—the story of What's Essential about the present moment in business—comes in the form of a tombstone. It's a tombstone that bears the epitaph that I most hope to avoid. To wit:

Thomas J. Peters
1942–Whenever
He would have done some really cool stuff ...
but his boss wouldn't let him

Meanwhile, I know exactly how I *do* want my tombstone to read:

Thomas J. Peters
1942–Whenever
HE WAS A PLAYER!

Not "He got rich." Not "He became famous." Not even "He got things right." Rather: "He was a player." In other words: He did *not* sit on the sidelines.

Agree or disagree with me on anything else, but you must agree with me on this: Getting off the sidelines—Being a Player—is Not Optional.

No. In fact, Being a Player is ... *Essential!*

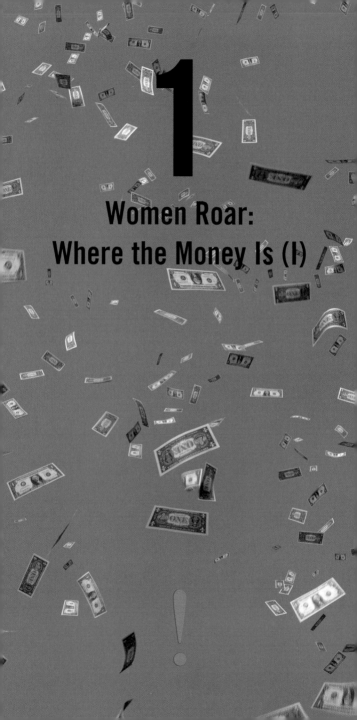

1

Women Roar:
Where the Money Is (I)

Contrasts

Was	Is
Equality for women: a moral issue (still true, but ...)	Equality for women: a business opportunity! (true ... more than ever)
Women buy, big-time (and men ignore that fact)	Women buy, big-time (and men *embrace* that fact)
Women spend men's money (still true, but ...)	Women spend their own money (true ... more than ever)
Women's incomes: a "supplement" to men's incomes	Women's incomes: rising faster than men's incomes
Business travelers are (mostly) men	Business travelers are (increasingly) women
Assumption: Men are the chief breadwinners of most households	Fact: Women are the "chief purchasing officers" of most households
Women tolerate male-oriented marketing	Women reward women-friendly marketing
Women are a "specialty" market	Women are *the* market
Women's-market "initiatives"	Women's-market strategy

!Rant

We are not prepared ...

WE (MALES) SNICKER about women's "shopping proclivity" but persist in **reflexively acting as if the "consumer"— for furniture, cars, food, and computers alike—is a "he."** • Or else we dice the market into micro-segments and treat women as **ONE "NICHE" AMONG MANY**. • Our organizations, meanwhile, are still **overwhelmingly male in the composition of their top management and boards of directors**, in their corporate culture, in their approach to product design and marketing. • **BUT WE MUST WAKE UP AND SMELL THE TRUTH: WOMEN ARE THE PRIMARY PURCHASERS OF ...** *DAMN NEAR EVERYTHING*. • We must, therefore, strive on every front to achieve nothing less than **Total Enterprise Realignment** around this awesome, burgeoning, astoundingly untapped market.

!Vision

I imagine ...

A car dealership ... **WHERE SALESPEOPLE UNDERSTAND THAT WOMEN BUY THE CARS** ... and where the entire approach to **marketing and merchandising and sales and service caters to** ... Women's Way of Being and Buying.

A hotel chain ... **THAT WELCOMES WOMEN BUSINESS TRAVELERS** with due consideration ... **with branding and operations that put an emphasis on connection, comfort, security, and other women's priorities.**

A WIDESPREAD RECOGNITION among business leaders of the **blazingly obvious ... that women are (like Willie Sutton's banks) Where the Money Is ... that women's earning power, their spending power, their role in purchase decisions (both personal and corporate) are all increasing at a breathtaking pace.**

Break of Day: I Begin to See the Light

18 December 1996.

At around 9 a.m. I enter the Boston HQ of Wordworks, one of America's 10 million women-owned businesses.

Donna Carpenter, owner of Wordworks, and thirty other women have gathered here. They own businesses. They've written books. Their combined net worth—including not a penny from trust funds or spouses—runs to tens of millions of dollars. (At least.)

I am here to ... listen.

I *do* listen.

I am staggered.

My life takes what amounts to a 90-degree turn.

I listen to these ... Incredibly Powerful Women ... dispassionately report stories of having been held in

My life takes ... a 90-degree turn.

contempt. Of having been made to feel invisible. Of having been treated as brainless.

By bank and bankers and investment advisors.

By auctioneers.

By car salesmen.

By doctors and hospital administrators and other healthcare personnel.

By hotel managers and clerks.

By airline managers and staffers.

By computer salesmen.

I am a "with-it" guy. In some ways, I do "get it." I marched in the giant pro-choice rally in Washington in 1989. I put the toilet seat down after I pee. I do my own laundry. (I even keep track of when the detergent is running out, and buy refills as necessary.)

And yet I learned ... in three short hours ... that at a fundamental level, I just didn't "get it."

I admit it. Reluctantly. I didn't know what I didn't know. (Didn't have a clue, actually!) Hence, over the last decade, my work in this area has been penance—an effort to "get it" (which I can do pretty well intellectually, but *never* emotionally), and become a ... Noisy Champion.

Not a champion for "women's rights." Many others have done that much better than I ever could. But a champion for ... OPPORTUNITY. The opportunity that exists ... AMOUNTING TO TRILLIONS OF DOLLARS IN THE U.S. ALONE ... if bankers and carmakers and hoteliers and healthcare providers "got it" ... and started to develop the products that women want, and started to deliver them and service them in ways that women would appreciate, or at least in ways that don't offend women.

I am here to ... LISTEN

trends

women roar!

THE APPOSITE SEX
Side note: I have become a champion of another opportunity that women present. Namely: the Huge Opportunity that would ensue ... if big companies (most of which are still led mainly by men) took advantage of the Leadership Skills of women in their ranks.

See the companion volume *Essentials: Leadership* for more on how women are ... Answer No.1 to the Leadership Problem.

Women's Day: I Hear Women Roar!

12 October 2000.

I walk into the Convention Center in Long Beach, California, early in the morning. I notice immediately that most of the men's-room signs are taped over. Now they say "Women." Why? Because this building has been taken over by the 2000 California Governor's Conference for Women. I was invited to deliver a keynote address at the conference by California's First Lady, Sharon Davis. Ten thousand "screaming and shouting and raving women," as a female friend put it, are surging—YES, SURGING—into the hall. (That's why the restroom designations have been changed.) The men present? The Governor's wife's husband (Gov. Gray Davis). A handful of other token males ... all bowing and scraping, and remarking on the matchless energy in the hall. And me.

I had come a long way in four years. Concerning this "women's thing," I'd gathered a ton of stories, a raft of data, and a full front-end loader's worth of conviction. So, scared to death by the enormity of the honor I'd had bestowed, I worked as hard as I've ever worked on my 40-minute speech to ... The Conference. I spent hours, literally, on just the opening PowerPoint slide. I called it "Statement of Philosophy." It read like this:

I am a businessperson. An analyst. A pragmatist. The enormous social good of increased women's power is clear to me; but that is not my shtick. My "business" is haranguing business leaders about my fact-based conviction that women's increasing power—leadership skills and purchasing power—is the Strongest and Most Dynamic Force at Work in the American Economy today. Dare I say it as a long-time resident of Palo Alto and Silicon Valley ... this is even bigger than the Internet!

The theme of the conference was "Celebrate the Past, Create the Future." And yes: Women have come a long, long way, baby! Yes, there was much to celebrate.

And yet ... there was (and *is*) a long, LONG way to go.

ECONOMICALLY CORRECT

My passion about this "women thing" is not about "political correctness."

It's true: I believe that the advances made not only by women, but also by African-Americans, are the two most important things that have happened in the United States during my 60-plus-year lifetime. These are Moral Achievements of the Highest Order.

However: I am not *in any way* on a Moral Crusade. I *am* on a Crusade. But it is a Businessman's Crusade ... against stupidity and lost opportunity ... against the economically short-sighted practices of the male powers-that-be.

I do not believe that most men are Sexist Pigs. I do believe that they (we!) are ... Oblivious Idiots.

The *Real* "Chick Lit": Horror Stories

I have collected hundreds of horror stories about women being dismissed or ignored in the marketplace:

A California State Senator with severe back and neck problems visits a renowned physician, and brings along her husband for moral support. Ten minutes into the conversation with the doc, she is forced to interrupt: "Excuse me, Doctor, but it's my neck that's in pain." (The doc had been talking exclusively to her husband about her problem.)

A woman who has a bank balance to die for attends a land auction in Kentucky. ("I was probably the only one in the room who could have bought anything that was up for bid by writing out a check on the spot," she tells me later.) Time and again during the initial two-hour session, the auctioneer fails to respond to her standard signals for recognition. At the first break, she approaches him and says, "Start recognizing me, or the next person you'll hear from will be my lawyer. He's very good."

A woman accosts me after I finish keynoting the First Annual MacDonald Communications Marketing to Women seminar, held in New York in early 1998. It's Kathleen Brown. Former twice-elected Treasurer of the State of California. Former Democratic gubernatorial candidate. Now she had become one of the top half-dozen executives at Bank of America.

"Tom," she says (we know each other from her gubernatorial campaign), "would you do me a favor the next time you're in the Bay Area?"

Me: "If I can, of course."

Kathleen: "I'd like you to have dinner with me and David Coulter." (Coulter was then CEO of Bank of America.)

Me: "Sure. Why?"

Kathleen: "I'd like you to tell him what you just told this group."

Me: "*Me?* You were Treasurer of the Earth's Sixth-Largest Economy, and considered by one and almost all to be a brilliant success. You're one of the half-dozen Most Powerful Women in one of the most powerful single

'nations' on earth, our dearly beloved Great State of California. I'm just a 'consultant.' Why me?"

Kathleen: "*He'll listen to you.*"

Story like that one … drive me batty. No: They … PISS ME OFF. BIG-TIME. And I just keep asking:

WHY? **WHY? WHY?**

CONSTRUCTION CRITICISM

One sign of modest progress: The horror stories occasionally come via men. Once, after an all-day seminar in which (as usual) I addressed the "woman's thing," a fellow approached me. Turns out that he was the most successful shopping-mall developer in the large American urban center where I was presenting that day.

"I must apologize," he began with a chuckle, "I was the one who burst out laughing at one point during your discussion on the women's issue. It got me thinking. I remembered a meeting last week. A bunch of guys—about 15 developers, architects, contractors, engineers, bankers—sitting around designing a shopping center. Every one of us was male! Every one of us! And the 'end users' will be overwhelmingly women. And it never occurred to us. In retrospect, how bizarre."

Indeed. How bizarre—yet (alas) how common.

Horrors! Clueless in Carolina

My wife is the CEO and Chief Designer of a successful home-furnishings company, headquartered in Vermont. Twice a year, she makes the pilgrimage to the giant furniture show in High Point, North Carolina. I usually join her for a couple of days as an accompanying spouse.

The furniture industry is out of it. (Understatement.) It's run almost entirely by old white males with manufacturing backgrounds. ("The future is wood, my boy.") The situation is pathetic. Especially when you consider that women buy, or make the key buying decision on, most furniture sold today.

But I hadn't quite got the *perfect* illustration of just how "pathetic." And then it came, courtesy of a mere advertisement in an industry magazine that puts out a

... run almost entirely by old white males ...

EMBARRASSING. STUPID. PATHETIC. DUMB. AWFUL.

daily publication during the show. It was a double page ad for a seminar that would take place as part of High Point extravaganza. Title: "MEET THE EXPERTS! How Have Retailing's Most Successful Stayed That Way."

Among the presenting "experts" listed, there are 16 ... MEN. I have an engineering degree. I did the math.

Women purchase about 94 percent of the product. (WOMEN ... REALLY AND TRULY DO RULE ... THIS INDUSTRY.) Hence, if there are 16 men presenting, and if men buy 6 percent of the product, there should be ... 251 women "experts" on tap.

No problem with that logic, eh?

The reality was slightly different. The actual number of women (of course):

ZERO.

Stupid.
Pathetic.
Dumb.
Awful.
Embarrassing.
(Alas, the folks who placed that ad probably weren't embarrassed in the least.)

CONCIERGE

... a hugely lucrative market ...

Horrors! Finding "Hostility" in "Hospitality"

From a 2002 *New York Times* report titled "One Woman's Account of Two Hotel Experiences":

"A female business traveler reports on a two-night trip she made recently to the Phoenix area:

" 'I stayed at two hotels, both Hilton properties, that could not have been more different in their accommodation of women,' she wrote in an e-mail message. Her impressions illustrate the challenges hotels confront in marketing to female business travelers, whose ranks are growing rapidly.

" 'The first hotel I stayed at was an Embassy Suites in Tempe,' she said. 'I'd reserved online and asked for a quiet room. When I checked in, the young woman at the counter greeted me by name and explained that she had set aside a top-floor room, and that no one was next door to me. She gave me information on the pool, the complimentary happy hour and the cooked breakfast in the morning.

" 'I went out for meetings. When I got back, the guest services manager had sent up a welcome box with two bottles of water, an apple granola bar, bite-sized cookies and a bag of blue-corn chips. The evening happy hour was social, with families as well as groups of businessmen. I wandered in for a draft beer, which I enjoyed by the pool as kids splashed around.

" 'The hotel had a Mexican restaurant where I went for dinner. The maitre d' seated me at a booth with no

trends

women roar!

"PORN" YESTERDAY?
In my seminars, I often use a slide with a black background and purple letters. To wit: "WANNA SEE MY PORN COLLECTION?"

My "porn collection" consists of photographs ... torn from the back of Fortune 500 company Annual Reports ... featuring Boards of Directors.

Typically, the board shot features 20 somber faces. Eighteen Very Old White Males. One woman. (HR?) One African-American. (Corporate Communications?) No, I am not asking for 51 percent women. (Or for 10 percent African-Americans, 14 percent Hispanic-origin sorts, and 4 percent Asian-

Americans. I'm actually not "into" quotas in any way, shape, or form.

But I am ... a business pragmatist. And I believe: If a Board does not resemble *at all* (AT ALL!) the market being served ... then something (Big) is (Badly) wrong.

raised eyebrows that I was alone. Later, my room was dead quiet, as promised, and in the morning after an early business meeting, I returned for a cooked breakfast omelet and tea in a cheery café setting with families and other single women travelers, as well as businessmen. It was terrific. I checked out content. The bill was $87.'

"Her other hotel was the Phoenix Airport Hilton.

" 'I got lost en route, so I called for directions from my cell phone,' said the woman, who didn't want her name used. 'Reception put me on hold for 3 minutes and 48 seconds, which I noted only because of the roaming charges. I hung up and had to call back.

" 'When I arrived I saw the problem: one clerk at the desk, and 12 customers milling around to check in. When my turn came, there still was a line behind me. 'Okay, you're in room 408,' he announced. Normally they do not publicly announce the room of a single woman, especially in a crowded lobby.

" 'My room was near the executive lounge, which was open for drinks and snacks from 5 to 7 p.m. I went in around 6:40, and there were 20 people, and only one other woman. The men were clearly well into their second hour there. A television was blaring, and the buffet snacks looked like a three-year-old had crawled across them. Cheese bits were scattered on the counter; tortilla

---

REALLY, I'D SETTLE FOR JUST A MINT

I was so pissed off. I was in a big hotel in London, preparing for a seminar. In the elevator was a picture of a woman guest under a lush duvet.

So what's the problem? Don't I believe that hotels should try to cater to women by featuring them in marketing material?

Well, this woman was no average "woman business traveler." She was a gorgeous babe,

about 25 years of age. In short, she was a man's fantasy of the surprise that he would love to find in his room. (I'm being honest here.)

During the seminar, I asked the female segment of my audience if I was wrong to deem that elevator advert blatantly offensive. Of the roughly 600 people at the gathering, over 40 percent were women. I could see that lots of the "guys" were taken aback by my

ire. But every (EVERY!) woman who had seen the ad thought it was stupid. Alas, most of the women also said, in effect, "But what do you expect?"

Is it any wonder that *91 percent* of women say, "advertisers don't understand us"? Or that *58 percent* go much further and claim they are downright "annoyed" by advertising pitches apparently aimed at them?

Meeting Expectations

Talk about "dumb"! Time was, the percentage of business travelers who were women was … well, *very small*. That figure now sits at roughly *50 percent*. What's more, many of those women business travelers are big-time "influentials." Women, for example, constitute the majority of CMPs. As in: Certified Meeting Planners. As in: people who book enormous blocks of hotel rooms!

In this area alone … tens upon tens of *billions of dollars* are at stake … each year.

crumbs were everywhere, and there was not a single piece of appetizing food that hadn't been mangled, except a very neat, untouched stack of raw broccoli florets. Let me tell you something: I would rather be in a buffet with a dozen 9-year-olds than with a half-dozen males in their 20s and 30s.

" 'The bartender asked me what I wanted. Several people looked. 'Umm,' I said, embarrassed, tired and a little defensive.

" 'We don't have Umm,' he said. I flushed and glared. I ordered a Coors Light and fled to my room, where I had a room-service cheeseburger.

" 'Bill for the room, with tax and dinner, was $170,' she concluded. Guess which hotel I'm going back to the next time? But let me ask you something: Do hotels really think about these things when they think of female travelers?' "

I've got dozens of stories of women being abused by hospitality companies. Arguably, only Wyndham, with its program oriented toward women business travelers, does much strategically to serve this hugely lucrative market

Note that word: "strategically." The problem is not that folks in the hospitality industry deny that there's "an opportunity" here. But they consign said opportunity to "tactical program" land, and can't imagine it becoming the basis for ... Wholesale Brand Realignment.

Horrors! Showroom Shenanigans

A smartly-turned-out financial services executive approached me after one of my riffs on women's treatment in the marketplace. Here's her "horror story." During her lunch hour a few days before, she'd gone to a Mercedes dealership with every intention of buying a car. All three salesmen were in their cubicles, eating sandwiches. (Yes, they were men. Do you even need to ask?) As she prowled the showroom floor, not one of these three guys bothered to acknowledge her. Finally, one guy finished his lunch and ambled toward her. First words out of his mouth: "Honey, are you sure you have the kind of

trends

women roar!

money to be looking at a car like this?"

Some men who read this remark will say, "Bullshit. She's making that up." Or at least, "She's exaggerating." (Indeed, that would have been my response before that ... Pivotal Day ... almost ten years ago.)

FACT: None of the women who read this will have that kind of reaction. None of them will even find the exchange to be at all exceptional. This is something that, after a decade of listening and study, I know.

FACT: I have a gajillion stories like this. From financial service companies. From hospitals and docs. From hotels. From computer companies. As well as those forever-silly car dealerships. And when I've told these stories, I've never ... NEVER ... ... NEVER ... among the tens of thousands of people to whom I've told them ... seen one woman shake her head in disagreement.

FACT: It is rare for me to speak on this topic ... and not have at least two or three women wait in line, often using up many minutes of their very precious time, to pass on yet another tawdry tale.

"Tom, here's another one for you ..."

"Tom, you won't believe this one, but ..."

Funny thing: I DO BELIEVE.

COMPANY CAD
True story: The female CEO of a UK financial-services firm goes to lease a company car. The salesman at the leasing agency greets her by saying, "I didn't know that [company name] was offering company cars to secretaries."

That women are grossly underserved in the marketplace might make sense—if it made sense. But it doesn't. *It's absolutely insane.*

The insanity results in part from what Martha Barletta calls the "poor story." Because of one statistic—that all women, on average, earn only 76 cents on the dollar compared with men—the Marketing Powers-That-Be assume that women are a less-important target for their efforts. Wrong!

What the "poor story" misses, per Barletta, is the "power story" about women that is right out there, hiding in plain sight. Women are *roaring*, ever louder ... in terms of earning power, in terms of purchasing power, in terms of their role in the home and in the workplace as the key decision makers on what gets bought.

What follows is a raft of data, much of it provided by Barletta, that amply supports ... the Women's Power Story.

Women bring in more than half of household income in 55 percent of U.S. households. Don't forget that 27 percent of households are headed by single women—and those women, of course, bring in *all* of their household income. Meanwhile, 30 percent of working *wives* earn half or more than half of their family's income.

Plus, the trend is aggressively moving women from the "poor story" to the "power story" side of the ledger. In an information-and-service-based economy, women are proving themselves to be uniquely qualified (and absolutely essential) participants. And they are being rewarded for their contribution ... the myth or reality of

trends

!

women roar!

"HIGHER" MATH

Another key element in the women's "power story": education. Women are coming to dominate higher education, in particular—both in attendance and in graduation rates. Already, woman in the United States earn 57 percent of all bachelor's degrees and 58 percent of all master's degrees.

And more education means more money. Men still dominate joint earnings in lower-education families, but women are gaining ground elsewhere. Among married women who have completed graduate school, for example, 43 percent earn more than their husbands.

Result: Families with highly educated women are ... where the loot is.

the "Glass Ceiling" notwithstanding. Thus, *between 1970 and 1998, men's median income rose by 0.6 percent, while women's median income rose by 63 percent.*

Holy smoke!

And talk about "power"! Already, women constitute 43 percent of Americans with a net worth of a half-million dollars or more. That's a whole lot of money for business leaders to be consigning to the "also-ran" pile.

Do the Math: Decisions, Decisions

And yet … And yet even those figures on women's earning power belie the true *spending* power that they wield. Because women are the sole or primary decision makers for just about every kind of household purchase. Big-ticket stuff as well as small household-goods stuff. In 85 percent of American homes, it is a woman who handles the checkbook and pays the bills.

They are the instigators-in-chief for most household buying, accounting for a mammoth *80 percent* of all spending by U.S households. In certain categories, moreover, their role in the decision-making process is overwhelmingly large. Their share of the total number of buying decisions tallies as follows in these areas:

Home furnishings: 94%.
Vacations: 89%.
Kitchen appliances: 88%
New homes: 75%.
Healthcare: 80%.

Among too many marketers, a myth persists to the effect that while women buy the "small stuff" (soup and soap and whatnot), men buy most of the durable, high-dollar items. Wrong! (Again.) To wit:

Computers: Women purchase 66 percent of all personal computers.

trends

women roar!

Consumer electronics: Women account for 55 percent of purchases.

Automotive: Women buy more than 60 percent of new cars, they buy 53% of used cars, and they influence 80 percent of all car sales.

Home improvement: Women initiate 80 percent of purchases relating to home (do-it-yourself) projects.

More on the latter category: What could be more of a "guy thing" than hardware and home improvement? In fact, Lowe's reports that 50 percent of customers who come through its stores are women. And Ace Hardware, in a recent study, found that women customers on average spent 50 percent more than male customers.

Holy smoke!

Big point: Just because men show more of an *interest* than women in, say, cars or computers or consumer electronics … doesn't mean that they buy more of that stuff. On the contrary. Yes, men may get a kick out of

Women are the instigators-in-chief of most consumer purchases.

THEY'VE COME A LAWN, LAWN WAY

A few years ago, after a speech that I made, a fellow came up to me. He'd attended a seminar of mine about three years earlier, when I was just warming up on this topic. He said that he'd initially dismissed my comments on the women's market ... but a little later, he decided to do "a little research." The results astounded him. He found that 80 percent of the buyers of his primary product are women.

That product? Riding lawn mowers.

kicking the tires at an auto showroom. But, more often than not, it's women who are making final purchase decisions and driving vehicles off the lot.

All the foregoing relates to women's (huge) role as "chief purchasing officers" within their households. But women also play a predominant role as professional purchasing officers for corporations and organizations. They now constitute 53 percent of buyers and purchasing personnel. Their "commercial spending power" also encompasses their majority status in HR departments, where they're responsible for (among other things) employee benefits decisions. And overall, they play a larger and larger role in influencing corporate decision making on whether to open—or not open—the organizational purse.

Add up all of the above, and the result is an American women's economy that accounts for more half of U.S. GDP. That is to say: around $7 trillion. (U.S. GDP is $11 trillion.) Hence, according to one wag, the world's largest economies could be ranked as follows:

Earth's third-largest economy: American men ... at, say, $4 trillion.

Earth's second-largest economy: All of Japan ... at about $4.3 trillion.

Earth's largest economy: American women ... at a whopping $7 trillion.

Do the Math: The 10-Million-Woman March

Want to hear women *really* roar? After years of mashing their heads against the corporate glass ceiling, they've begun to say ... almost in unison ... GO TO HELL.

Sure, there has been a modest increase in the number of female Fortune 500 CEOs. (And a more-than-modest increase in the publicity that women like Sara Lee's Brenda Barnes and eBay's Meg Whitman receive.) But the real story is that in the United States alone there are *10.6 million* women-owned businesses. (Definition: companies in which women account for at least 50 percent of ownership.) Women-owned enterprises employ 19.1 million people. That corresponds to ... one out of every seven American workers. In fact, women-owned businesses employ more workers *inside* the U.S.A. than the fabled Fortune 500 employ *worldwide*.

Scoreboard ...

Women: 1

Fortune 500: 0

In total, American women-owned businesses at last count tallied about *$2.5 trillion* in revenue. To put that in

RETURN TO SPENDER
From an email that I received in response to one of my talks on the burgeoning women's market: "I make one-third more money than my husband does. I have as much financial 'pull' in the relationship as he does. I'd say this is also true of most of my women friends. Somebody should wake up, smell the coffee, and kiss our asses long enough to sell us something! We have money to spend—and nobody wants it!"

SCOREBOARD:

WOMEN:

1

FORTUNE 500:

0

THE POPCORN STAND: MARKETING AS IF WOMEN MATTERED

Go to your local Borders or Barnes & Noble. On the burgeoning "Business" shelves, you'll find 25 books, maybe twice that number, on Six Sigma or some other version of the "Quality Thing." And yet I believe ... with TOTAL CERTAINTY ... that the "Marketing to Women Thing" is FAR BIGGER than the Quality Thing. It is the biggest imperative today for companies that seek growth and profitability. (Again, just ... Do the Math!)

So why are there so few books on Marketing to Women? That question flabbergasts me. I don't know the answer. But I do know one thing. On the ridiculously short list of books on this topic, two titles stand out: Marketing to Women, *by Martha Barletta, and* EVEolution: The Eight Truths of Marketing to Women, *by Faith Popcorn and her collaborator, Lys Marigold.*

In the next two chapters, I will pass the authorial baton to my friend and colleague Marti Barletta, who will discuss ... more fully than I can ... the ins and outs of How Men and Women Are

Different … and How Companies Can (and Must) Appeal to Women.

But under no circumstances should you neglect Faith Popcorn's book. It is an absolute must-read. Buy it. Study it. Internalize its "Eight Truths" … eight Big Ideas for attracting women's custom. Herewith, I'll briefly discuss just one of those Truths … desperately hoping, of course, to pique your interest in the other seven.

(See also the Cool Friend interview with Popcorn, page 44.)

Truth No. 1: Connecting Your Female Consumers to Each Other Connects Them to Your Brand. *"The Connection proclivity in women starts early,"* Popcorn and Marigold write. *"When asked, 'How was school today?' a girl usually tells her mother every detail of what happened, while a boy might grunt, 'Fine.' "*

In my seminars, after using a PowerPoint slide that shows that quote about the roots of the Connection Proclivity, I always ask the same question: "Is there anyone in this room who disagrees with that characterization of the difference between boys and girls?" I leave plenty of space for people to object. I welcome their objections. I have yet to get a single objection.

For each of the eight "truths," Popcorn and Marigold proffer advice to would-be would-be women-friendly companies. Regarding the Connection Proclivity, for example: "What if ExxonMobil or Shell dipped into their credit card database to help commuting women interview and make a choice of car pool partners?" And: "What if American Express made a concerted effort to connect up female empty-nesters through on-line and off-line programs, geared to help women re-enter the workforce with today's skills."

Indeed. What if companies did those sorts of things? More important: WHY THE HELL DON'T THEY?

proper perspective: *The revenue from American women-owned businesses exceeds the GDP of Germany ($2.4 trillion)!*

Start looking at this stuff, as I have been doing now for well nigh a decade, and you'll be positively stunned. Stunned—and then outraged.

"Outraged" because: Women as purchasers, professionally and privately, are responsible for more than half of all spending in the U.S. economy. And yet:

trends

women roar!

Financial services companies ...
don't get it.
Health services companies ...
don't get it.
Hospitality services companies ...
don't get it.
Computer companies ...
don't get it.
Automobile companies ...
don't get it.

NONE OF THEM GET IT.

(Or so, alas, it seems.)

The Guru Gap

I despise the designation "management guru," but if such a designation has any validity, then I guess I am one. There are probably about 20 of us who are lucky enough to be in the top tier. I'm not sure how many there might be in the next tier. But I'm sure of one thing: There are damn few management guru-esses. And I'm even more sure of something else: There is not *one* male management guru other than me who has focused—in any way, shape, or form—on the "women's issue."

The point is not that I'm proud of that. (Though, to be perfectly honest, I *am* proud of it.) The point is that I'm befuddled by it: WHY HASN'T ANYONE ELSE ... AMONG THIS AWESOMELY SMART BUNCH ... ADDRESSED THIS HUGE OPPORTUNITY? (Or even written, literally, a single word about it?)

WHY? **WHY? WHY?**

Well, I am determined. I'm going to push this "women's thing." And I'm going to piss some people off in the process. (I HAVE ALREADY PISSED OFF ... A LOT OF PEOPLE. AND LOST A FAIR AMOUNT OF BUSINESS. "FORGET IT, HE'S JUST GOING TO BEAT US OVER THE HEAD ABOUT THAT DAMN 'WOMEN'S STUFF.'") But I'm

trends

women roar!

GLOBAL GAL-FEST

Most of my thinking on the Women's Thing, and most of the research I've gathered on the subject, relates to the fully developed Western world

But I've found that my "women's riff" translates remarkably well.

Case in point:

The plane landed in Kuala Lumpur. Eighteen hours before I was scheduled to put on an all-day seminar. It was late 1998, and I'd been extending and polishing that "women's riff" for a couple of years.

But now I was in Asia, and in a Muslim-majority nation on top of that. I guessed only 10 percent or so of the seminar participants would be women.

So I asked myself: Should I drop the women's chapter?

I decided not to. And I'm very happy about my decision. I did use some sandpaper, and removed some burrs here and there. But otherwise what I offered was my "straight" pitch.

I was right on one score. Only about 10 percent of participants were women. But I have seldom received such a heartfelt response as I did from this vocal minority. Almost every woman approached me, and thanked me for giving them a voice.

Did I change the world that day? No. Or not by much. But I did increase my resolve not to pull my punches, regardless of my map coordinates.

pushing it ... dear male executive colleagues ... because, in the words of bank robber Willie Sutton, "That's where the money is." Money that comes from effectively developing products and services and experiences that respect and serve women in every industry: from automobiles to health care, from financial services to information technology.

Going to China; Or, Hear *Me* Roar

Nixon went to China. Only an old Red-baiter could have pulled it off. I'm a junior member of that same league. An Old White Male (OWM). Two tours in Vietnam. Swear

like the sailor I once was. A guy's guy. And yet I'm dead square stuck on this ... Women's Thing.

If nothing else, it has led me to some amazing encounters with amazing women.

Media superstar Linda Ellerbee, one of my all-time heroines, approached me at a reception following the Fifth Worldwide Lessons in Leadership Teleconference, the biggest show of its kind (Management Town Hall) on earth. Linda was the host-referee of the show, which featured three OWMs: Ken Blanchard and Stephen Covey, both over 60, and Youthful Tom Peters, age 58 at the time. Linda—the Toughest Dudette *or* Dude in Any Damn Town!—not only gave me a hug, but teared up. WHY? "Thank you, thank you for doing the 'women's thing,'" she said. "Coming from you makes all the difference."

After a speech in Hong Kong to a meeting of top managers from SC Johnson, the giant consumer-goods company, I headed for the streets for some of that city's fabled shopping. (I am the shopper in my family!) As I approached the hotel's front door, an elegantly turned-out professional woman accosted me and thanked me effusively and emotionally for doing the "women's thing." She said that she was, if I recall correctly, the first working mom ever promoted by her company to corporate VP. And in saying what I said at that meeting, I had offered "public confirmation" from a Respected Old Male for her achievement.

In short, I've been blown away. By incredible stories. By hard, cold facts.

By the immensity of this opportunity. By the degree to which "we" (by which I mean "men") have neglected it.

trends

women roar!

By the extent of the emotional response I have elicited from hard-nosed, successful businesswomen.

Hey, I'm having the time of my life with this issue! I intend to stick the needle in OWMs as often, as deeply, and as painfully as I possibly can! I think it's a hoot to watch them squirm! (And to watch a few of them—Big Wigs, especially—turn beet-red with ire.) And I know that ... for those who can stop squirming, for those who can contain their vainglorious anger

... the payoff numbers collectively will be in the ...

TRILLIONS
of dollars.

"TURNAROUND TOM"?

I've never wanted to be a CEO. Reason: Too damned hard!

But I admit I have gotten the itch ... for the first and only time ... as a sole and direct result of getting on this "women's shtick."

I would love (LOVE!) to be CEO of (say) a large financial services corporation ... for exactly 60 months. I would take that enterprise, dig into its every nook and cranny, and redirect its strategy ... by 179.5 degrees ... in the direction of developing products for, marketing them to, and distributing them to women.

For starters: I guarantee that at the end of those 60 months, 11 out of 20 members of my Board of Directors, and 13 out of 20 members of my Executive Committee, would be ... women.

(Oops, maybe I am into quotas, after all.)

TOP 10 TO-DOs

1. *Seize the day.* Do as I did: Carve out a day, gather women you know (both personally and professionally), and let them give you a piece—*many* pieces—of their mind.

2. *Hit the books.* Read all about it. ("It" being the women's market.) Read Popcorn. Read Barletta. Most business books are bunk. Not so when it comes to this … roaring opportunity.

3. *Listen up.* Ask women about their experiences with your company. Don't just ask, "Are you satisfied?" Find out what you aren't doing—but *should* be doing!—to tailor your offering to women's needs.

4. *Speak truth to (male) power.* Speak up. Speak out. Don't be afraid to trumpet the Women's Thing to all and sundry.

5. *Follow the money.* Really follow it … by gender. Examine where buying power truly lies, and how buying decisions are truly made.

6. *Defend difference.* Accept and honor the ways that women are different—VERY different—from men in how and why they buy.

7. *Get "personnel."* Hire women. Lots of them. To market to women, you need to have women around—in *leadership* positions.

8. *Let the word go forth.* Convey the message—*in no uncertain terms*—that condescension to women is verboten. Do it through training and retraining, as necessary.

9. *Pink-slip the clueless.* Simply fire those who will not learn to respect women—and, likewise, the women's market. For example, any salesman who ignores women must be … shown the door.

10. *Let "ladies" go first.* Make Appealing to Women your No.1 marketing priority. The old way: Women are a "gender of last resort." Turn that assumption upside-down. Remember: Women, not men, make the market go 'round.

COOL FRIEND: Faith Popcorn

Faith Popcorn, best-selling author of **The Popcorn Report** *(1990) and* **Clicking** *(1997), is the founder of BrainReserve, a marketing and strategy consulting firm. One of the world's leading trend experts, she identified and presented to the world such major long-term trends as "Cocooning," "Cashing Out," and "Anchoring." Below are remarks that she made about her book* **EVEolution: The Eight Truths of Marketing to Women** *(co-authored with Lys Marigold, 2000).*

* *

I thought about the fact that we work with all these Fortune 500 companies, and they think they're marketing to women—who buy 80 percent of the products and control 80 percent of the money—but they're not. They're not talking to women. They don't know how to talk to women. Just like they have no clue what to give their wives for their birthdays. They really don't realize that women have a separate language and a separate way of being. And the problem has been that it's been so politically incorrect to say that.

I started to really study it. I met with Natalie Angier who wrote *Woman: An Intimate Geography* and also with Helen Fisher, author of *The First Sex: The Natural Talents of Women and How They Are Changing the World.* Helen Fisher talks about how women think. Helen calls women's thinking process "web thinking," which came from the cave days. When women had to watch the baby and watch the mountain lion and cook and everything else, their peripheral vision got very strong. That's how women receive messages, peripherally. And women's brains actually fire off left-right, left-right. Men, on the other hand, went out and walked straight ahead ... hunted for something, and dragged it back. Men's brains fire off "A-A-A-A-A," and I don't mean to make this simplistic, but they run the world this way. Men's brains actually fire off left-left-left, right-right-right. Men's brains and women's brains work differently. It's a fact.

* *

There are smart guys, of course. But the guys who respond to this view do not run Fortune 500 companies— yet. I got a message from the chairman of a multi-, multi-, multibillion-dollar global company, and I know him really well. He said, "Dear Faith: I distributed this book to my female executives. Thank you." I wrote to him, "Dear X: This book is not about marketing *for* women, it's about marketing *to* women." And he wrote me back about how ungrateful I was. He'd bought 14 copies at full price! Can you believe it?

* *

It's not like people fall down at my feet about all this. It's not like people are saying, "You're so right, we've got to do this." We had to sell this thing so hard. We shoved these case histories down the throats of corporate America. It's tough. ...

[T]he most successful case history in the book is Jiffy Lube. We went in, studied the situation. We realized that women are driving their cars in. They're the ones who are taking care of the car and changing the oil. Women take care of this maintenance. We told the Jiffy Lube people to stop screaming at these women when they drive in— it scares them. You know how these guys come out from under the hood of the car yelling about "Change this, replace that!" It's scary because these guys are so loud.

Our suggestions: Escort her out of her car, put her in a clean waiting room, put some toys in there for her kids, put some music in there, let her have access to email if she wants, let her read some magazines—current ones, please!—and give her a clean bathroom with the seat down and a changing table. Add some low-fat snacks, and you've got her for life. ...

Jim Postl—he's chairman [of Jiffy Lube] now—he is different. He's rolling this right out to 100 shops.

* *

How come there are no drinks for women? Why isn't
there a soft drink for women? It does not exist. There'
Diet Coke, but it doesn't sell for women. A drink reall
designed for women, not just positioned [to them].
Something that has minerals, vitamins, or a strategy
in it intrinsic to the brand that's really for women—nc
just a cute, hot commercial. Does not exist. So many
opportunities waiting out there.

* *

[O]ne morning I got up and thought, "Omigod, look a
all these women working at home." ... So we sent out
a couple of thousand cameras, and we said, "Take a
picture of your home office and send it back to us." /
... all the home offices had flowers. All the home offi
had a place for an earring, because women take off th
earrings when they talk on the phone. I noticed that a
the women working behind their desks crossed their l
They had pictures of their kids on a corkboard.

And I decided to make Faith Popcorn's Home Offi
Cocoon. I went to Hooker furniture, and I licensed it.
They sold $5 million worth the first day at High Point
Furniture Market in North Carolina. ... It's not brain
surgery. I'm not in the furniture business. But I thoug
let's see if I can license this. Boom!

* *

I went to Detroit. I went to this big car company. I sai
"Look at these Eight Truths." So the top guy sends m
to the director of marketing. ... I go in there, and [the
director of marketing] says, "What? Blacks, Hispanics
gays—now women? Another advocacy group? I don't
need this. We sell enough Explorers to women. We
don't need to sell anymore." And I say to him, "You'r
missing the point. You can retain these women foreve
for generations." And he says, "Oh, come on." That w
it—end of meeting. I went to a Japanese car company
and they said "We don't thread the needle that way."
That's the thinking out there. It's very typical.

* *

[A] woman [says] to a guy, "How come you didn't know what to get me for my birthday?" And he says, "How am I supposed to know?" And she says "I left the catalog on the bed." A guy would just brush the catalog right off the bed. A woman, if she saw a catalog on the bed, would think, "That wasn't there this morning. What's that?"

* *

[I often hear] a male marketer, marketing to the male supermarket owners, telling us—and I've heard this in meetings no less than ten times—that they believe that women socialize at the supermarket. Every time I hear this I have to ask, "Do you know any women?" These guys imagine a world in which women take their two kids to the supermarket, the kids meet each other, and the women socialize. Who ever heard of such a thing? These men have some *Stepford Wives* vision of the world. It's absolutely insane. I've never met anyone who hasn't been in a rush to get out of the supermarket.

* *

[W]e say over and over again, "Have you ever taken your female employees out for a drink? Have you ever said it's okay for them to tell you what's the matter, what's going on, what they feel?" Hang out with a woman.

If the supermarket manager actually bothered to shop with a woman, he'd understand her issues. Just follow her, and watch her roll the cart out to the parking lot, see the struggle of rolling the cart next to the car, [when] the cart bumps into the car and scratches it. And then dealing with the bags of groceries. They're heavy. She lifts them out of the cart and into the back of the car. Then the kids. They're not light, and they've got to be put into the safety seat. And they don't want to get in their seats. And then there's the ethical dilemma of "Should I bring the cart back to the store, or do I just leave it out here in the middle of the parking lot?" And it's hell. ...

Hang out with your subjects. Hang out with the people you're trying to market to. And not in a fake environment like a focus group room.

2

Women Roar:
The Difference
Is Real

By Martha Barletta

Contrasts

Was	Is
Market to men (because men and women aren't all that different)	Market to women (because an appeal to women will reach men, too)
Being "on top" ... of the social pyramid	Being "in tune" ... with one's peers
"Me first"	"Me, too"
Things and theorems	People, people, people
Humor: Laughing At	Humor: Laughing *With*
"Show me respect"	"Build my *trust*"
Transaction	Relationship
"Just the facts, ma'am"	"Tell me a story, sir"
Solution ("Fix it")	Understanding ("Feel it")
Details: "Superfluous!"	Details: "Super! Fun!"
"Forget it—it's in the way"	"Let's do it—it's on the way"
Short attention span	"Longer list"
A good solution	The perfect answer

!Rant

We are not prepared ...

We trade stories, during our off-work hours, about **THE DIFFERENCE BETWEEN MEN AND WOMEN.** We joke about it, we complain about it, we accept it as a fact of life. • In a business context, however, we persistently—and foolishly—shun any recognition of the distinction between male and female gender cultures. **We slice the market into various niches and segments,** and target those groups in specially designed marketing campaigns. And then **WE SHY AWAY FROM MARKETING TO WOMEN** in a way that appreciates their approach to thinking and feeling, buying and shopping. • We worry about "alienating men" if we make an appeal to women. **But we must begin worrying instead about how thoroughly we have alienated women by ignoring their particular sensibilities.**

!Vision

I imagine ...

A widespread acceptance, especially among the marketing powers-that-be, that **WOMEN'S WAYS OF THINKING** ("we" rather than "me") and connecting ("peer" rather than "pyramid") form **the attitudinal background against which profitable marketing campaigns will be built.**

A NEW EMPHASIS in advertising on the use of language and imagery that appeals to **women's sense of commonality,** rather than men's focus on competition.

An accommodation of women's quest for **"THE PERFECT ANSWER,"** not as means of targeting women as a "niche," but as **a holistic approach to marketing that will improve companies' overall competitive position**—and draw in men as well.

We're mostly alike. But ...

Of People and Things: Across a Great Divide

Like Tom, I believe that the best way to teach and to learn is through storytelling. So let me start with a story.

One day my husband came home from work and said, "So, Marti, I had lunch with David today."

I said, "Oh, great. How are David and Nancy doing?" David and Nancy had been very good friends of ours for many years.

"They're getting a divorce," my husband said.

"Oh, no. What happened?"

"I don't know."

My response: *"You don't know? Didn't you ask him?"*

"Well, of course not," my husband said. "If he'd wanted me to know, he would have told me."

Guys have an invisible barrier against getting too personal. They believe that when you get too personal, you're being intrusive. You're invading the other person's private space. And they actually don't want to "go there"—because, for them, "there" is just a morass of emotional mess that they don't want to get involved with.

Women, though, believe that the *people* elements of a situation are *the good part*. They want to know all of the details. They want to discuss all of the underlying meanings.

Quite simply, women are more people-focused than men. For them, ultimately, it's all about people. Whereas men think that people are *important*—but hardly ever all that *interesting*. What interests men are things and theorems: concrete things like cars and computers, on the one hand, and abstract, conceptual stuff, on the other.

That is just one of the very real differences between men and women that I will describe in this chapter.

Of Mice and Men: Two Genders, Two Cultures

How, exactly, are men and women different?

Think of it this way: Before scientists test any new medical treatment on human beings, they test it on mice. At first glance, that seems a little odd. But it turns out that mice and human beings share *99 percent of their DNA*. Scientists

TOM SAYS ...

HE SAID, SHE ... LISTENED

Marti's book is among the very small set of my favorite books on the topic of gender difference. Another is Why Men Don't Listen & Women Can't Read Maps, by Barbara Pease and Allan Pease. It's based not on anecdotal evidence, but on the latest findings from neurobiology—and it's amusingly written, to boot.

Consider:

"It is obvious to a woman when another woman is upset ... while a man generally has to physically witness tears or a temper tantrum or be slapped on the face before he even has a clue that anything is going on. Like most female mammals, women are equipped with far more finely tuned sensory skills than men."

More: "A woman knows her children's friends, hopes, dreams, romances, secret fears, what they are thinking, how they are feeling ... . Men are vaguely aware of some short people also living in the house."

The point: As a species, we simply haven't advanced much since our cave-dwelling days. In that epoch, guys were either "on" or "off." They got up, pre-dawn, and went out on a danger-filled hunt; their adrenaline surged. They spent the day pursuing game, came in at dusk—and promptly fell asleep. Men, the biological research reveals, are either all the way "on" ... or in a resting state, (that is, 30 percent "on"). Women, meanwhile, are responsible for defending the family, the cave, the community ... all the time. Thus, women are never "off": Their "resting" state is 90 percent "on."

"As a hunter, a man needed vision that would allow him to zero in on ... targets in the distance," the Peases write, "whereas a woman needed eyes to allow a wide arc of vision so that she could monitor any predators sneaking up on the nest. This is why modern men can find their way effortlessly to a distant pub, but can never find things in fridges, cupboards, and drawers."

More: "Female hearing advantage contributes significantly to what is called 'women's intuition' and is one of the reasons why a woman can read between the lines of what people say. Men, however, shouldn't despair. They are excellent at ... imitating animal sounds." (!)

have confirmed that strange-but-true fact through genome sequencing. So despite all the obvious differences—size, skin versus fur, tail versus no-tail—it all comes down to a genetic difference of 1 percent.

That's how I think of the difference between men and women. We're mostly alike. But that "1 percent" difference can manifest itself in a powerfully big way.

Are all men categorically one way, and all women categorically another way? Of course not. We all know that just because on average men are taller than women, that doesn't mean that every man is taller than every woman. Nobody is typical on every point. However, a huge mass of research now shows that the bell curve for men is in one place and the bell curve for women is in another place. This research comes from a wide variety of fields: anthropology, biochemistry, neuroscience, socio-linguistics.

Here, I'll be making my argument mostly through stories, including stories about my own experience. But every point that I make has ample science to back it up. As a matter of fact, scientists are finding that gender differences are hard-wired into our biochemistry, hard-wired into our brains, hard-wired into the hormone systems.

(Quick example: Some studies indicate that women physically experience emotions more strongly than men do. In MRI tests, PET scans, and CAT scans, you can actually see certain areas of the brain light up in response to various inputs. And research studies show that women's brains glow more brightly than men's brains do in response to certain emotional experiences.)

trends & the difference is real

TOM SAYS ...

TALK IS DEAR

The novelist and former *New York Times* columnist Anna Quindlen: "I only really understand myself, what I'm really thinking and feeling, when I've talked it over with my circle of female friends. When days go by without that connection, I feel like a radio playing in an empty room."

I have shared that remark with audiences that included tens of thousands of men. Again and again, I ask, "Can you imagine—in any way, shape, or form—any *man* ever making that remark?"

We all agree: No way!

Message. We are not worse. We are not better. We are different. And the impact on enterprise strategy is enormous. Or ought to be.

The upshot of those differences is the difference in what I call "gender culture." No marketer would launch a product into a different ethnic culture—say, the Hispanic culture—without first learning something about that culture's language and customs. So it is with marketing to women. They have a different gender culture from the one that businesspeople are used to addressing.

The idea of gender culture may seem counterintuitive. After all, boys and girls grow up in the same households together. They have the same mothers, the same fathers. How can they possibly grow up in two different gender cultures? Yet men and women are as different as Indiana and India. A difference of just two small letters—and you have two places that couldn't be more different. (Again, think of that 1 percent difference in DNA.)

Note in particular: Differences in gender culture cut right at the heart of marketing. These are differences in priorities, in preferences, in communication styles, in decision processes. If those aren't the things that affect how consumers make buying decisions, I don't know what is.

Women Think "Peer," Men Think "Pyramid"

Just about every time my husband and I go out to dinner with another couple, there comes a moment when the guys play Show-and-Tell.

One of the guys will bring out the newest cell phone, for example. He'll say, "You know, with this new cell phone, I can sit on the train and download all my stock quotes right here on the screen."

And someone, usually one of the women, will say, "Oh, do you do that a lot? It's kind of hard to read that little screen."

"Well, no. But it's cool. I could do it if I wanted to."

It's all about having the power, having the latest technology—and having it first, before other guys do. For guys, it's all about showing that you're ahead of the pack.

Here's why: When men look at a social structure, they see a hierarchy. They view everything in terms of a pyramid. And at the back of their mind, there's always an ingrained sense

&

Men and women are as different as Indiana and India.

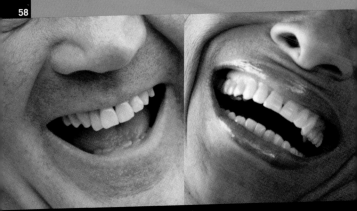

Men's humor and women's humor

of what the pecking order is among the individuals in that pyramid. Women, though, tend to see a social structure as more like a peer group—as flat rather than hierarchical.

If you see yourself as operating in a hierarchical society, then obviously your job as an individual is to seek superiority. So men are more oriented than women toward establishing an advantage over others. Women, conversely, are more oriented toward emphasizing equality and fairness. Instead of seeing win-lose opportunities, they see win-win opportunities.

One way that this difference plays out is that men generally care more than women about being right. In disputes within couples, for example, there's usually a point at which the woman decides that she's invested all that she cares to invest in the discussion. She'll say, "Okay, honey, you're right." But that won't be the end of it. Not for the man. He'll come back the next day with a book or something else that lets him say to her, "See, it says right here that I was right yesterday." "Okay, fine. You're right," she'll say. She'll let him be "right"—not because he necessarily is right, but because being "right" matters so much more to him.

Some other ways that this difference plays out:

Women Think "We," Men Think "Me." For men, the core unit of society is the individual. It's "me." For women, it's "we." They see themselves as part of a community ("we") that extends out from "me" in a series of concentric circles: "me

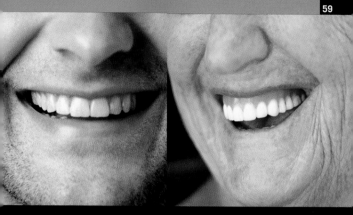

are different by 180 degrees.

and my immediate family," "me and my extended family," "me and my neighbors," "me and my coworkers." Wherever they go, women carry between their ears a whole collection of peoples' priorities and preferences.

Women Want Trust, Men Want Respect. Men have a deep need for others to respect them, to look up to them. Women, by contrast, generally don't want to be put on a pedestal. They don't want to be looked "up to" any more than they want to be looked "down on." They want to be looked "across at." So for them, the operative dynamic is really one of trust between equals rather than "respect."

Women Affiliate, Men Differentiate. If you are, foremost, a "me," then you've got to be different from all the other "me"s, right? That's why men are more oriented than women toward differentiating themselves from other people. Who has the bigger muscle car? Who has the more powerful technology? With women, it's more about affiliation: "Look how much we have in common with each other!"

Women Laugh With, Men Laugh At. Men's humor and women's humor are different by 180 degrees. Male humor, operating in a hierarchical mode, is built around the putdown: "Look at that guy. What a dweeb!" Women's humor isn't about laughing *at* someone. It's about laughing *with* someone: "Oh my gosh, that's just the way I am. That's just the way it is in our house."

Women connect through commonality.
Men connect through competition.

Men Connect Through Competition …

Modes of connecting. This is a big one. Let's take it in two parts. (We'll let the men go first.)

Men connect with each other through competition. That shouldn't be surprising, given what we've discussed so far, right? It's very consistent with the hierarchical male gender culture. A typical example of how men relate to each other: A bunch of guys go out and play football or baseball. They try real hard to beat each other. One team wins, the other team loses. Everybody has a good time. Afterward, they have beer and pizza.

But even in a casual, unstructured setting, you'll see men connecting to each other primarily through competition.

One researcher did a series of focus groups with men. But the real research took place in the waiting room, before the focus group. The researcher wanted to see how a group of guys who didn't know each other would start to talk with each other. And you know what? For a really long time, with each group, there would be silence. The guys' attitude: "What's the point? I didn't come here to talk with a bunch of guys I'm never going to see again."

Finally, somebody would break the silence. One guy would say, "Oh, man, I am so tired. I stood outside Tower Records for eight hours last night, waiting to get that new Rolling Stones album that just came out." And a second guy will say, "Oh, yeah? I got that album, too. As a matter of fact, I have every Rolling Stones album ever made. I've even got some of their bootleg stuff." And a third guy says, "You know what? I met those guys backstage last year, and they were totally cool."

TOM SAYS …

ANOTHER VOICE: NO WOMAN IS AN ISLAND

I am an unabashed "difference" feminist. There is no doubt in my mind that men and women are equal. There is also no doubt in my mind that men and women are … *different*. And the difference is profound.

Consider the work of Harvard psychologist Carol Gilligan, author of the classic study *In a Different Voice*. Herewith, a brief summary of that brilliant and meticulous book:

- Men want to get away from authority and family. Women want to connect.
- Men are self-oriented. Women are other-oriented.
- Men are rights-oriented. Women are responsibility-oriented.

Point, counterpoint, score! One-up-manship. That's how guys exchange information with each other. That's how they get to know each other. For men, every conversation is a mini contest of sorts, with each guy aware of who came out ahead on each interchange.

I remember, when I started out in the workplace, I would go into a meeting and one of the men there would say something like, "So, Barletta, did you lose that big account yet?" At first, I would wonder: "Why is he jumping on me like that? I can't believe he said that to me." But now that I understand male gender culture, I know that such a remark is meant to be friendly. It's a way of saying, "You're okay. I see you as a buddy."

trends

... Women Connect Through Commonality

Instead of connecting through competition, women connect through commonality. Just as men have competitive games, so women have commonality "games." Here are three of them:

The "Me, Too" Game. Almost reflexively, two women talking together will reinforce what they have in common by "playing back" each other's most casual remarks. One woman says, "Oh, I'm telling you, I was trying to get my son to pick up his socks this weekend. Can't be done." The other woman then jumps in immediately, without even thinking about it: "Yeah, I can't get my son to pick up his socks either."

the difference is real

TOM SAYS ...

READING BETWEEN THE (GENDER) LINES
I love the writer Anita Shreve. Last year I read her magnificent novel *The Weight of Water*. No one else—and definitely no male—deals so lucidly with the painful tangle of what's called human relations. Simple fact: Women appreciate complex human relationships. Men are clueless.

Certainly that's true in the world of fiction.

Women's characterizations of both men and women are subtle and complex. But in 9 out of 10 cases, even among honored authors, male characterizations of women are mostly male *fantasies* of women. And when a female character is an admired professional, she is invariably described (admiringly, to be sure) in male terms—as "tough," "steely-eyed," and so on. It's hilarious.

Upshot: Men cannot "get" women. Period.

Men approach and deal with the world in a linear way. No twists. No turns. Little reflection, little attachment. Get the facts. Act. Move on. Let the chips fall where they may.

Women see bends and twists and reversals in every path that involves the interplay of humans. Women appreciate and live for those bends and switchbacks.

Or: "Traffic was terrible this morning."

"Yeah, I had terrible traffic, too."

There isn't much content in those messages. But for women, they function as a mini support mechanism.

The Scoop Game. Whenever someone seems in danger of being embarrassed, women will step in and try to "scoop" the person out of that situation. Once, at a conference, I was looking for something (a phone booth, or a bathroom). I came rounding a corner very abruptly, and almost ran into a brick wall. I felt like an idiot. So I looked around to see if anybody had seen me. A couple of women were standing there, and immediately one of them said, "Oh, everybody's been doing that." And another woman jumped in and she said, "Yeah, I almost did it myself."

Now, what it if it had been a couple of guys standing there? Would I have gotten the same responses? I don't think so. If the guys hadn't known me, they would probably just roll their eyes and continue with their conversation. And if they were friends of mine, they would say something like, "Walking into walls again, Barletta?" And that would be their way of being friendly.

The Life Story Game. Guys don't get this game at all. In the middle of a perfectly serious business meeting, one woman will look at another women and say, "That is the nicest necklace. I'm always looking to see what you wear, because you have the best taste in jewelry."

ANOTHER VOICE: WOMEN MAKE "CONNECT" CALLS

Judy Rosener, writing in *America's Competitive Secret: Women Managers*: "Women speak and hear a language of connection and intimacy, and men speak and hear a language of status and independence. Men communicate to obtain information, establish their status, and show independence. Women communicate to create relationships, encourage interaction, and exchange feelings."

TABLES—OR TALES?

A few years ago, the editorial director of the UK's Redwood Publications—which puts out mega-circulation company magazines for the likes of Boots and Volvo—patiently explained to me which kinds of articles work for men and which kinds work for women: Men "need" (NEED!) "tables, comparisons, rankings." Women want "narratives that cohere."

trends

&

the difference is real

The second woman will not just say, "Thank you" and continue with the conversation. Instead, she'll say something like, "Oh, you know where I got this? I was on Cape Cod last year with my sister. We were visiting my parents for Thanksgiving. We were walking down the main street in Harwich, and I saw this in the shop. I just thought it was so pretty. But, you know, I'd just bought a really expensive black purse at another shop. So I thought, "Well, no, I really shouldn't." And then my sister gave this necklace to me for my birthday. Wasn't that sweet?"

Meanwhile, the guys at the meeting are thinking, "Come on, lady. Get to the point." But for the women, that story *is* the point. As they see it, the details are the good part. They're sharing information about each other; they're connecting.

Women Seek Understanding, Men Seek Solutions

Another difference in male and female communication styles—one that most men say they know all too well—involves women's need to be "understood."

Every book on gender differences has some version of this story: A woman comes home from work. She says to her husband or her boyfriend, "What a day I've had! My boss gave me two more projects. She knows that I already have three that are due next Wednesday. My coworkers were supposed to get material to me yesterday. Nothing—haven't seen a thing. I don't know how much longer I can take this."

What does the husband or boyfriend do? He's a good guy. He wants to be supportive. She's brought him a problem. So

---

TOM SAYS ...

PEASE UNDERSTAND ME!
More insights from Barbara Pease and Allan Pease:

"Women love to talk. ... Men talk silently to themselves."

"Women think aloud. ... Women talk, men feel nagged."

"Women multitrack."

"Women are indirect. ... Men are direct."

"Women talk emotively, men are literal. ... Men listen like statues."

"Boys compete, girls cooperate."

"[M]en hate to be wrong. ... [M]en hide their emotions."

Concerning that last point, the Peases add: "When a woman is upset, she talks emotionally to her friends; but an upset man rebuilds a motor or fixes a leaking tap."

he tries to solve it. He says, "You know what you should do, honey? You should tell your boss that you can't take those new projects unless you get deadline relief on the other one. Tell your coworkers …"

But it's no use. The woman doesn't want *solutions*. (She's smart; she'll figure out what to do.) She wants *understanding*—the feeling that he's "there" for her.

A scenario like this one occurred with my husband and me during the first year of our marriage. He said, "Marti, I hate to see you so upset like this. Why don't you quit?" Now, he was trying to be supportive. But I looked at him and I said, "*What are you talking about?* Quit? No way. I'm just venting here."

For women, just having someone appreciate what they're going through discharges a huge amount of negative energy. Not so with men. When they come home after a tough day, they don't want to talk about it. They want to go into their den and close the door. And they'll let you know when they're fit for civil society again.

Women Get Personal, Men Stay Detached

When men are making connections with each other, they are very reluctant to share personal information. (Think back to that conversation about David and Nancy's divorce.) Instead, they speak in terms of facts and actions: sports, current events, gizmos, and gadgets.

Women's gender culture is much different. Women will get personal in what strike men as the least personal of situations.

Women get personal.
Men stay detached.

Consider a man and a women each going to shop for a car.

The man will go into a dealer's showroom and say, "I'm looking for a sedan. I need such-and-such horsepower. I need four-wheel drive. I need this or that amenity inside." Just the facts. Just what's on the spec sheet.

The woman is likely to launch into a version of her life story: "You know, I need a really nice car, because I'm a realtor and I have to drive my clients around in the car. Of course, I also have to take the kids to soccer practice all the time, so my car has to have plenty of room in it. And we go to the beach every weekend. You would not believe how much sand that dog can track into a car." The salesman, if he's a man (and he probably is), will say, "Yes, Ma'am, and what kind of car are you looking for?" And she'll think (and may or may not say), "Weren't you listening? I just told you what kind of car I'm looking for!"

Details, Details: Women See More

Women can drive the men *crazy* with details. You ask a woman, "Do you prefer black or white?" For women, the only reasonable answer to that question is "It depends." It depends on the context. Are you talking about apparel? Home décor? Women need to know, *in detail*, how that choice—a choice as simple as black-or-white—will figure in their lives.

Men, however, see it as beneath them to get involved in minor details. They prefer to process information at a "headline" level. When they're making a decision, they do their best to stay focused: "Let's get all this messy, obscure detail out of the way. Let's just focus on what's important here—the skeleton of the situation, the three or four key points, *the big picture*."

trends

&

the difference is real

TOM SAYS ...

SHOPPING TALK
Back in 2002, I came across an article in the *Charleston* [West Virginia] *Gazette* that had this headline: "Shopping: A Guy's Nightmare or a Girl's Dream Come True?"

For boys, the paper reported, it's "buy it and be gone."

For girls, it's "hang out and enjoy the experience." One source for the article, Antaun Hughes of Capital High School, put it this

way: "Women enjoy going through the actual process of everything, while guys like to get straight to the point."

At least some folks (*young* folks) "get it."

But with women, "the big picture" means something completely different. How can you understand the big picture unless you really dig into it? Women insist that you can't look at just one thing at a time: "How are we going to use this product? Who is going to use it? If I buy *this* product, then I can't buy *that* product. Who will be affected by that decision?"

All of this has a basis in men's and women's hard-wired traits. Men can see better from a distance, whereas women have better peripheral vision. Similarly, a scientist at the University of Chicago, Joan Meyers Levy, has found that women possess a finer gauge for isolating and distinguishing between details. Here's an example to illustrate her finding (it doesn't match her actual experiment): If you give a man and a woman each a stack of 50 cards and ask them to sort the cards into appropriate groups, the man is likely to sort the cards into 5 piles of 10, while the woman is apt to create 10 piles of 5. She sees finer gradations of detail—finer levels of differentiation—among the items to be sorted.

Women will admit that if they're not

Women Do It All at Once, Men Do One Thing at a Time

Men prefer to do things in a linear fashion. They like to focus on one thing at a time, do a good job at it, and then move onto the next thing. Women prefer to tackle several things at a time, moving each of them ahead on a parallel path. As a matter of fact, many women will admit that if they're not multi-tasking, they start to feel uneasy.

Take me, for instance. Say that I'm at the stove, cooking dinner—stirring soup, maybe. If I'm only stirring soup, I'll look around for something else to keep me busy. I'll sort the mail. I'll return a phone call. I'll get my daughter started on her homework. I'll get my son started on doing the dishes. Now I'm using my time in a way that works! After all, I need to stir the soup only every 30 seconds. That leaves a full 28 seconds in between stirs that I can fill with other tasks.

Men get a little nervous when too many things are going on at once.

One day my husband said to me, "Marti, I'm going over to the Walgreens."

So I said, "That's great, honey. Would you return that rental movie to the Blockbuster next door?"

"I'm not going to the Blockbuster."

"Why not? It's next door."

"Marti, how come every time I go out, you have to pile on some extra thing for me to do? Can't I just go to the Walgreens and get what I wanted to get?"

"But, honey, it's on the way."

For men, such a task is never "on the way." It's always "in the way."

multi-tasking, they start to feel uneasy.

Men see multi-tasking as a formula for allowing lower-priority tasks to intrude on high-priority tasks. Women don't see it that way. They see multi-tasking as a smart, efficient way to get a lot of things done.

TOM SAYS ...

USING "SENSES" DATA: ADVANTAGE, WOMEN
In her book *Marketing to Women*, Marti discusses several ways in which women are physically "hard-wired" to be different from men.

For example:
Vision: Men, focused. Women, peripheral.
Hearing: Women's discomfort level is half that of men's.
Smell: Women have a more acute sense of smell.

Touch: The *most* sensitive man is less sensitive to touch than the *least* sensitive woman.
People orientation: By age three days, baby girls exhibit twice as much eye contact as baby boys.

trends

the difference is real

&

Women Maximize, Men Prioritize

The Saturday night fights. I'm not talking about boxing. I'm talking about the little ritual that my husband and I enjoy just about every Saturday night.

We'll be preparing to go out, and he'll say, "So, Marti, are you ready to go?"

And I'll say, "Yep, I'm ready."

He'll then go into the garage and sit in the car. Five minutes later, I come out. He's fuming.

"Marti, what is *wrong* with you?" he asks. "Why do you say you're ready to go when you're not ready to go?"

"Nothing's wrong with me. But to get to our garage, I have to walk through our kitchen. And I am psychologically incapable of walking through our kitchen without putting the bowl in the dishwasher, putting the cereal back in the cupboard, and wiping up the counter on the way. It's on the way." (Again: *on the way.*)

He just shakes his head.

Simply put, men prioritize—and women maximize.

Say you gave Jack and Jill each the same list of five tasks, ranked in order of priority. The mission: Come back at the end of the day with these five tasks done. Typically, Jack will come back with the first task done—positively, completely done. He might also have the second task done. But very likely, he won't have finished the other three tasks; tasks 1 and 2 simply take up all his time and energy. Jill, meanwhile, might come back with the first task left undone. But she'll have completed tasks 2, 3, 4, and 5. Maybe those four tasks are clustered in one part of town, whereas task 1 has to be done somewhere else entirely.

TOM SAYS …

A DIFFERENT VOICE: WOMEN WRITE CIRCLES AROUND MEN
Helen Fisher, writing in *The First Sex: The Natural Talents of Women and How They Are Changing the World:* "The [Hollywood] scripts that men write tend to be direct and linear, while women's compositions have many conflicts, many climaxes, and many endings."

CARGO CULT?
Marti notes this copy in an ad for *Cargo*, a recently launched shopping magazine for men: "Shop like a man. Read it, club it, drag it home."

That's the male mentality. Says it all, doesn't it?

Jack will look at Jill and think, "You know what? She didn't even get the most important thing done. She can't focus." And Jill will look at Jack and think, "Oh, the poor dear. He can only focus on one thing at a time." Both gender-based judgments have a grain of truth, but neither of them does anything to help us communicate better.

A Longer List: Women Want More

Several years ago, when I was buying my first cell phone, I asked my husband to help me pick one. I don't enjoy shopping for technology, but my husband is a chief technology officer, so he was happy to help me out. I said, "Thanks, honey. Now here's what I want. Because I'm traveling coast to coast a lot, I want to be able to roam without having to worry about roaming fees. I'd like a small phone, because I'm already schlepping around a lot of stuff and I don't need any extra weight. Plus, I'd rather have a phone without one of those little antennae sticking up out of it; that would just get caught on everything in my briefcase. And you know what else? Those little Motorola phones are adorable. I would love it if I could have one of those." So off he went.

A few days later, he came back and said, "What you need is AT&T Digital One Rate Service."

"Great," I said. "And what kind of phone do I get?"

"I don't know. Whatever comes with that."

"Honey, it was very manly of you to listen so well to only the first thing that I said. But I actually did care about those other things, too."

At that point, he basically threw up his hands and left the matter for me to figure out. So I got on the AT&T site. I found out that one of the phone options there let you choose from various colored face plates. Among the choices was a lovely color called ocean blue, which really took my fancy. I spent a lot of time locating a dealer that had a phone with that face plate in stock. And then I drove 45 minutes out and 45 minutes back to get that ocean-blue cell phone.

I showed it to my husband. He said, "My goodness, Marti. I had no idea that the color of the phone was the most important thing to you."

trends & the difference is real

"Honey," I said. "Color is not the most important thing. It's the *least* important thing. But if I'm going to all this trouble, why should I get something that's only 85 percent of what I want, rather than something that's 100 percent of what I want?"

The message here: *Women have a longer list*.

People ask me, "Do women look for different things in a product than men do? What do women look for in cars that's different from what men look for in cars? What do women look for in computers?"

Indeed, women do look for some things, or care a bit more about some things, than men do. But in the main, women want all the same things as men want—and then some.

They don't stop at just the "most important" stuff. They care about the stuff that's lower on their list—the details that help them establish a more holistic context for their buying decision. They're willing to go that extra mile to get something that's 100 percent of what they want. To women, the details matter. (In my cell-phone purchase, the color of the phone was the least "important" element in my decision. Yet it was also the factor that determined which brand I finally chose.)

The good news for marketers is that details are what give you a chance to distinguish yourself from your competitors. These days, at the level of what's "most important," most products are highly competitive with each other. It's lower down the list of product attributes—lower down that "longer list" that women carry around in their head—that true differentiation becomes possible.

Women Want "the Perfect Answer," Men Settle for "a Good Solution"

Here's the crux of it all—the difference in gender cultures that sums up most of the other differences: When making a decision, men look for *a good solution*, whereas women look for *the perfect answer*.

Let's look at this issue in terms of marketing, shopping, and how people make buying decisions. (Again, I'll delve more deeply into that area in the next chapter.)

For men, shopping is about solving a problem: "I need such-and-such. Here are the three or four key specifications for satisfying that need. I'll find something that meets those criteria, and then I'll be done. Next stop, Priority No.2." Women, by contrast, discover what their buying criteria are only in the midst of shopping. For women, figuring out what they want is what shopping *is for*.

A hypothetical case: Jill and Jack each go out to buy a pair of black slacks.

Jack goes out with three criteria in mind: He wants the slacks to be permanent-press; he wants cuffs; and he wants to spend less than $80. His likely course of action will be to head straight for the store where he buys all of his other clothes, and to buy the first pair of black slacks he sees that meets those three criteria. Mission accomplished. Now he can go home and watch sports on TV.

Jill, instead of focusing on specific product features, will have in mind an ideal context for the black slacks: "I wish I could find something to wear to that office party on Friday." She'll go to one of her favorite shops, take five or six pairs of black slacks into the dressing room, and try them on. And that's where the decision-making process—which is also a

trends & the difference is real

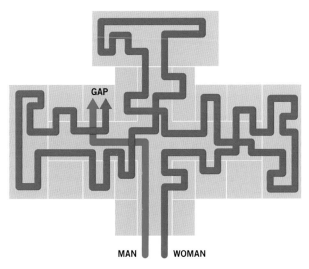

GAP

MAN | WOMAN

Mission: Buy a Pair of Pants

learning process—begins. Let's say that each pair fits her perfectly. Nonetheless (and this drives men up the wall), she will put every pair back where she found it. Her thought process runs as follows: "This pair is great; it doesn't wrinkle, so it will pack really well, and I do travel a lot. But this pair is a bit dressier, which means that I can wear it not only to the office party but to fancier parties as well. And this third pair is cut so that my legs look thin in it, and I like that. Hey, you know what would be really great? What if I could find a pair of black slacks that was wrinkle-free, had a bit of a dressier look, and made my legs look thin? And what if it was on sale? …" So she sets off to find what she has now identified as the *perfect* pair of black slacks.

Not long ago, I found the perfect visual representation of this difference. It's a funny little graphic that shows separate male and female pathways for traveling through a shopping mall in accordance with a very simple "Mission": "Buy a Pair of Pants." The male path, illustrated with a blue line, has a guy going straight from the entryway of the mall to the Gap, where he spent $33 on a pair of pants. Time elapsed: 6 minutes. The female path, shown in red, is a line that zigs and zags throughout the entire mall, taking the woman in question to almost every store in the place. Time: 3 hours and 26 minutes. Money spent: $876.

Obviously, this woman was seeking the perfect answer. Plus, on the way, she saw many other things that piqued her interest. Note that phrase, yet again: *on the way*. As she walks through the mall, she's thinking, "Oh, that's right, I also need to get a new pair of shoes. Oh, that's right, I meant to get a belt. Oh, that's right, the baby needs a new outfit." Which leads us back to another facet of female gender culture—the

---

TOM SAYS …

HOW MEN BUY
There is no more astute researcher of purchasing behavior than Paco Underhill. Consider this series of insights from his book *Why We Buy*: "Men … seem like loose cannons. … Men always move faster …. through a store's aisles. Men spend less time looking. … They usually don't like asking where things are. … You'll see a man impatiently move through a store to the section he wants, pick something up, and then, almost abruptly, he's ready to buy. … For a man, ignoring the price tag is almost a measure of his virility."

&

Men are simple.
Women are not.

"we" mentality. She's thinking, "My husband needs this. My kids need that. You know what? My neighbor said she was looking for a pair of red gloves. I bet she would love this pair." And so on.

What Women Want, Men Also Want

The difference between men and women is real. Real—and profound. Another visual representation of this difference that I like shows a pair of control panels. One, labeled "Man," features only a simple On-Off switch. The other, labeled "Woman," features that same switch, along with a whole panoply of dials. For a while, I hesitated before using this graphic in my presentations. I worried that it might insult men to brand them as being so simple. But when I asked my husband about it, he said, "What are you talking about? Of course we're simple, and proud of it."

Yes, relatively speaking, men are simple and women are not. And there's no justification for saying that one gender culture is superior to the other. They're very different, yet they're both equally valid.

But if we take that difference seriously, we'll see that the implications for marketers are momentous—even revolutionary. People often say to me, "This is great, Marti. Now I understand a lot more about women, who are the primary buyers of what we sell. But years ago, men were our primary customers. Doesn't focusing on women run the risk of alienating our male customers?"

Not at all. Companies as different as BMW and Merrill Lynch and Wyndham Hotels have found that when you improve your marketing to women, your customer satisfaction goes up among men as well. Marketing to women doesn't alienate men. It *attracts* men. Remember, men just want the "most important" stuff, while women have that "longer list." When you meet the expectations of women, you generally exceed the expectations of men.

Consider those male and female control panels. Both have an On-Off switch. If you can turn all or most of the dials on the women's panel, as well as flip that switch, you can fully activate both gender cultures in your favor.

trends
&
the difference is real

TOP 10 TO-DOs

1. *Be her equal.* Cast your pitch to women in peer-to-peer terms—rather than top-down terms. In other words, forget "pyramid power," and embrace *people power*.

2. *Join her.* Treat women as members of a mutually *inclusive* set. Remember: You're selling to a "we," not to a "me."

3. *Humor her.* Use humor to show what people have in common (laughing *with*), not what separates them (laughing *at*).

4. *Play her game.* Learn the rules of the communication games that women play—the "Me, Too" game, the "Life Story" game. Then design your marketing game accordingly. ("We, Too," anyone?)

5. *Lend her an ear.* Listen. Listen closely. And then (but only then) go into sales mode. If you show a woman that you understand her problem, she will let you help her solve it.

6. *Contribute to her story.* Place your brand in the context of the narrative that women weave about their lives. Ask: How can your company become a "character" in that tale? Then tell *your* story.

7. *Catch her "on the way."* Support women's penchant for getting the most out of her every movement. A surefire way to maximize sales: Help women maximize their efforts.

8. *Show her more.* Take advantage of women's wide field of vision. For women, no detail is too small or too "peripheral." So give them lots of options, lots of side benefits, lots of ways to buy from you.

9. *Listen to her "list."* Explore the "longer list" that women bring to every purchase. Your goal: to deliver "the perfect answer."

10. *Reach him, too.* Stop worrying that your efforts to reach women will be a turn-off to men. In fact, the opposite is more nearly true: If you "surprise and delight" women, you will attract men as well.

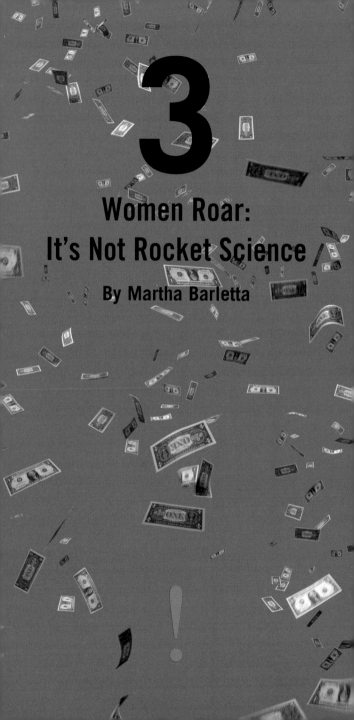

3

Women Roar:
It's Not Rocket Science

By Martha Barletta

Contrasts

Was	Is
"Pink" branding—for women only	Think "branding—for all"
Condescending to women	Catering to women
In the showroom: in the product	Outside the showroom: at point of purchase
Show the product	Show your face
Make the customer feel like a "winner"	Make the customer feel "warmer"
Inform the customer (focus on the "top line")	Immerse the customer (fill in the total picture)
Get him when ... "he's ready to buy"	Reach her while ... "she's here"
Men design, unthinkingly, for men	Men and women design—with women in mind
Stress to impress	Prepare to compare
Soothe his ego	Save her time
Marketing to men: Hard sell	Marketing to women: Easy money

!Rant

We are not prepared ...

We simplistically assume that because **WOMEN ARE COMPLEX** (in comparison with men), marketing to women must be complex as well. • We tie ourselves in knots as we go about tying little pink ribbons around some special "women's brand"—when, in fact, **the key to reaching women is to honor their complexity,** not to emulate stereotypes of female gender culture. Yes, our response to the "Women Roar!" challenge requires a big change of perspective. • But we must understand that it does not require a mammoth exertion of brainpower or a massive infusion of cash. **IT'S NOT ALL THAT DIFFICULT. IT'S NOT ALL THAT EXPENSIVE.** • And we must not let our fear of that challenge keep us from **acting fast to profit from this immense opportunity (one that everyone else is neglecting).**

!Vision

I imagine ...

A car dealership that honors women's emphasis on *context* and *comparison* within **THE BUYING PROCESS**—a dealership whose salespeople seek to learn **the entire *story* that underlies each customer's automotive needs.**

A FINANCIAL SERVICES FIRM that builds its business not around the prospect of frequent commissions (a formula that works only if customers are trigger- and trade-happy men), but around **the long-term goals and sensibilities of women.**

A retailer that designs its advertising around people, its physical spaces around **BUSY-WOMEN-WITH-KIDS-IN-TOW**, its product selection around women's "longer list," and its business model around **generating referrals from happy (women) customers.**

trends

&

it's not rocket science

Don't Paint the Brand Pink

Too many companies, having recognized that the women's market is big and that women are different from men, respond by trying to create overtly "female-friendly" brands.

Don't do it. *Don't paint the brand pink.*

I almost always advise against launching products or services designed specifically for women: a mutual fund "for women," a car "for women," a computer "for women." For one thing, women don't usually want different features from those that men want. For another thing, women will run away from a "women's brand" just as fast as men will. Here's why: Long experience in the marketplace has taught women that a "women's product" will usually be just a dumbed-down or more expensive version of what is sold to men. Let's face it: Women pay more than men for haircuts. They pay for alterations in clothing stores, while men generally don't. Women do not want to be told that something addresses their "special needs." That's condescending. It's alienating. And, of course, it does you no favors with men, either.

Yes, women are different from men. The difference is real, and it's big. And marketing to women requires real changes in how you do business.

But please, don't overreact. Marketing to women is not rocket science. It's not that hard. And, very importantly, it's not that expensive. To reach women, you don't need to paint the brand pink. Nor do you need to spend any additional money. You just need to change the way you're spending it, so that your efforts come into alignment with how women think and behave and shop.

Bottom line: Marketing to women is absolutely the easiest and fastest way to boost the return that you get on every marketing and sales dollar in your budget.

In this chapter, I will set forth a number of easy-to-grasp, easy-to-implement lessons on how to move in that direction.

The Invisible Woman: Stages of the Sale

First, though, let's cover a few basic—but easy-to-miss—points about how women operate within the marketplace.

One of the key reasons why companies fail to reach women is that they grossly underestimate the range and depth of women's role in the purchase process. Especially with big-ticket items, the assumption is that men do the buying. In fact, if you look closely at how couples and families actually make buying decisions, you'll see that while men play a rather prominent public role, women prevail in the less visible (but no less important) aspects of the process.

Almost every sale unfolds in five stages, and companies focus far too much on the one stage in which men dominate (or seem to dominate).

Stage 1: Initiation. In most couples, it is the woman who sets the buying process in motion. A couple may be talking about buying a new car, for example ("Yeah, we should get a new car one of these days")—but usually it's the woman who says, "Let's go out and visit dealerships this weekend."

Stage 2: Research. Remember, women have a "longer list" than men; they care about more details than men do. So they have a much greater investment in learning the options for any given purchase. Result: Women do most of the up-front

trends & it's not rocket science

research on products. They go to their husbands and say, "Here are the three car models that we should look at." Thus, she has already eliminated dozens of other models from the couple's consideration.

Stage 3: Face-to-face interaction. Here is where men come to the fore. When a couple goes to a store or showroom, men do most of the talking with the salesperson. Nonetheless, as I discuss below, women play a larger role at this stage than you might think.

Stage 4: Maintenance. That involves maintaining the product or service—and maintaining the relationship between buyer and seller. Since women handle the checkbook in most households, they are the ones who deal with problems relating to bills and statements, as well as with product or service problems. It's the woman who you'll hear say, "I can't read these statements. This is just not worth it. We're not going to use that company anymore," or, "Whenever I call that company, I can never get a live person on the line."

Stage 5: Aftermath. Because women invest more time and energy in the initial buying process, they also have a bigger emotional investment in a sale than men do. So when the woman in a couple is happy with a sale, she (rather than the man) becomes the kind of brand champion who can really help a company. After all, in many industries, sales is all about referrals. And in insurance, for example, one study shows that a woman will provide 28 referrals over her lifetime as a customer, whereas a man will provide 13 referrals.

trends

&

it's not rocket science

TOM SAYS ...

DUMB MOVE:
KING BLOCKS QUEEN
Marti shows how, stage for stage of the sales process, women are the customer. So why don't we talk about sales in that way?

Steve Farber, a colleague of mine, sent me an email a couple of years ago. He'd done a Google search, typing in two things: "Customer is King" and "Customer is Queen." The results:

"Customer is King": 4,440.
"Customer is Queen": 29.
Dumb. Dumb. Dumb.

... the invisible woman ...

Showroom Showdown:
What's Really Going On

Let's go back to Stage 3. Say that a couple visit a showroom
to buy a car. A salesperson, who is likely to be a sales*man*,
approaches them. The man in the couple takes the initiative in
dealing with the salesman, who in turn focuses on addressing
the man's concerns. What's wrong with this picture? Nothing,
necessarily. It's a very common scene. What's wrong is how we
tend to interpret that picture.

The woman may well be out to buy a car for herself. Or
she may be the intended primary user of the car. And even
if she's not, her influence at the other four stages of the sale
process make her a key player. So why does she let the man
do most of the talking? All kinds of reasons. One, she knows
that historically men get better treatment from salespeople
than women do. (Research studies show that even men agree
that male customers fare better than female customers with
sales personnel.) Two, she wants the man to handle necessary
negotiations. She knows that the competitive nature of male
gender culture makes that task less onerous for him. Three,
when it comes to evaluating the technology side of a product,

the man probably cares more about that stuff, and she appreciates his help on that front.

Female gender culture leads women to be openly solicitous of men's concerns—even when they will be making the final decision. A woman will turn to her husband and say, "So what do you think, honey?" Many salespeople misread that signal. They think, "See, I told you. He's making the decision." But that's really just a courtesy call. She is asking for his "buy-in" to her decision.

Similarly, women are not comfortable with directly contradicting the men in their lives in front of a third party. They don't want to come across as the shrewish wives of henpecked husbands. So they will often withhold their opinions in front of salespeople. But guess what? Those opinions still matter, and a woman will make them known to her husband later. By then, of course, the salesperson has lost the chance to address her concerns.

So even at this stage, salespeople need to take women seriously. They need to go out of their way to ask women what they think: "So, Marti, is that what you're looking for? Is there anything else you'd care to add?" That way, a woman can express her opinion without contradicting or embarrassing her husband. More generally, salespeople should listen more than they talk. Let a woman ask questions. Let her tell you her life story. That's how you will learn what her priorities are— what will help both members of the couple reach a decision.

Telling and Selling: Customers for Life

Marketing to women doesn't entail a "harder sell" than marketing to men. But it does entail a longer sell. And the rewards are well worth the extra effort.

You know why? Because every woman prospect that you convert into a customer will bring you wave after wave of new business in the long run. Again, a happy woman customer generates referrals at an amazing—and an amazingly profitable—rate. Women's highly deliberative decision-making process results in especially strong brand loyalty. And their tendency to "connect through commonality" causes them to spread that loyalty through classic word-of-mouth marketing.

"ROARING" SUCCESS (I): WOMEN AS INVESTORS

Here's another nuance of what Marti calls "female gender culture," one that relates directly to women's "slow to decide, loyal to their decision" approach to shopping and buying: Women are better investors than men. Consistently better.

Bottom line: Their penchant for making an emotional investment in their buying decisions (as well as a big time investment) translates into … superior financial investment.

In 1997, the National Association of Investors calculated investment-club returns by gender composition, as follows:

Women-only clubs—17.9 percent

Mixed clubs—7.3 percent

Men-only clubs—15.6 percent

In 2000, Value Line reported on the top investment clubs in each state, and then categorized the winning clubs by gender composition. (The reason for the total of 49: Vermont and Maine are not included; the District of Columbia is included.) The results:

All male—8

Co-ed—19

All female—22

Women Beat Men at Art of Investing," *reads the headline to an article in the* Miami Herald *that reported on a study by Professors Terrance Odean and Brad Barber, of the University of California at Davis. In the study, women outperformed men as investors. Reason: Men typically move "in and out" of a stock. They love "the game" of investing way too much. Women choose more carefully. They focus on achieving a secure future for their family, and they're more apt to invest for the long haul.*

Jane Bryant Quinn, in a Newsweek *magazine column echoes that point: "[W]hy all this focus on women and our supposed lack of investment guts? A far greater problem, it seems to me, is trigger-happy speculation, mostly by men. The kinds of guys whose family savings went south with the dot-coms. Imagine a list of their money mistakes. 1. Shoot from the hip. 2. Overtrade their accounts. 3. Believe they're smarter than the market. 4. Think with their mouse rather than their brain. 5. Praise their own genius when stocks go up. … 6. Hide their mistakes from their wives."*

Alas, the male-dominated financial-services industry still burdens women with … "not-so-easy terms." Rosanna Hertz, chairwoman of the Women's Studies Program at Wellesley College, says this about investment advisors: "I feel like they've never understood me and never will understand me. They talk in a masculine language. It's 'how risk-averse are you?' It's not a language I think in."

Little things matter to women

Here's an example: I'm a big fan of Peapod, the online grocery-delivery service. One time, during a visit from Peapod, the delivery guy handed me a beautiful bouquet of red roses. I said, "Oh, I didn't order any bouquet. I wish I had, but I didn't." Then he said, "We know that. But we decided this year that all of our customers who have deliveries scheduled on Valentine's Day should get a free bouquet of red roses." Wow, you can imagine my surprise and delight. And I told a lot of my friends about that little gesture, because it was so out of the ordinary. I still have a warm spot in my heart for Peapod, no matter how many times it might be out of stock on something in the future.

Little things matter to women, and women will talk about them among friends. Women's conversation is largely about exchanging personal anecdotes from their daily lives. When something good or something bad happens, that piece of information will transmit through a community of women much faster than it would through a community of men. To the extent that word-of-mouth—or "buzz marketing" or "viral marketing"—works with men, its power will be far, far greater with women.

A few savvy marketers are taking word-of-mouth to an even higher level—by moving from "tell a friend" to "sell a friend." Procter & Gamble, for example, launched a new cleaning product called Swiffer several years ago. When I bought my first Swiffer mop, I opened the package, and inside

and women will talk about them among friends.

was a coupon not just for refills but for another complete mop kit. At first, I thought, "Why are they including that? I just bought a mop kit." Then I thought, "Well, I really like this product. I bet my friend Jenny would like one, too." So I passed the coupon along to her. In effect, P&G had given me a reason to talk to Jenny about this new product that I liked.

Generate People Power

Perhaps the biggest lesson to take away from an understanding of female gender culture is that women thrive on people power. They want to get their consumer information from people. They want to see that the companies that they patronize care about people as well. They want to see and interact with the people in those companies.

A number of years ago, when the cell-phone business was still relatively young, Sprint did a study of how it was merchandising its phone options. Back then, its retail outlets generally displayed various phones behind glass walls; next to each option would be one of those "Take One" pockets with brochures inside. The study found that men loved that form

TOM SAYS ...

WORD OF MOUTH? DO THE MATH
A major stockbroker told me he has oriented his practice toward female clients—with great success. A research nut, he reports that his average male client recommends him to 2.6 others. On the other hand, his women clients recommend him to 21 others. Yes, that's two-point-six versus twenty-one.

Holy smoke!

Put people on your packaging.

of merchandising. They would come into a store, pick up some brochures, read up on products, make a decision, and then step up to the counter and buy a phone. Women, though, would walk right past those glass walls, find a staff person at the back of the store, and start asking questions. Initially, Sprint hadn't prepared staff members to handle customers in that way. But it learned to adapt its store layouts and staffing criteria to accommodate women, who have become an ever-higher percentage of its customers.

Two other quick thoughts on applying people power:

Put people on your packaging. Most companies still gravitate toward using a close-up picture of their product—be it a bowl of cereal or a laser printer. But why not use shots of actual people using the product in the context of their lives? Linking your company to real people is something that women find very engaging.

Give your Web site (and your company) a human face. Post photos and short profiles of your senior executives—or, indeed, of your customer care people. Don't hide behind an electronic wall. Women want to see who you are.

People-ize Your Communications

I worked in advertising for about 10 years. One phrase that I frequently heard colleagues use, almost like a mantra, was "product as hero." Now, the approach conveyed by that phrase might work if men are your only target. But it falls flat with women. To reach women, you should put people—and people-centered values—at the heart of all your consumer communications. Here's how:

Show real people, not ideal people. Most women don't identify with supermodels. Yet companies continue to feature the likes of Cindy Crawford in their ads. I'm not sure why. Personally, I don't care if Cindy Crawford recommends such-and-such a camera. Even if I bought that camera, I know I wouldn't have much in common with her. Instead, I want to see the kinds of people whom I recognize as being relevant to me.

Oil of Olay, in its advertising, does a good job of showing attractive but realistic-looking women in settings that most women can identify with. Its ad might show a woman sitting on the floor in her living room, with newspapers scattered all around her. Sure, it looks messy. But sometimes my house gets messy, too. I don't live on Planet Perfect, and neither do most consumers.

Immerse the customer. When I was in advertising, I learned to construct an ad around two or three "top line" points: Focus on the headline, make the case quickly, get in, get out. Again, that works with men—not so with women. To understand a product fully, women require immersion in the whole experience of that product.

Recently I saw an ad for a car that aligned with male gender culture perfectly: "Horsepower increased 17 percent. Torque increased 6 percent. Bragging rights increased 100 percent." Along with that text was a single, clean, beautiful image of the car. Guys get it, and move on. But a woman will look at that ad, turn the page, and forget it two seconds later. She needs something richer, something more complex, something with a real sense of context.

Think "warmer," not "winner." Men like to see themselves as winners—which explains the approach that one sees in a lot of advertising. In ad after ad, the point is to help consumers feel superior to others, or to help them incite envy in others. Even for something as prosaic as macaroni and cheese, aspirational, "be a winner" advertising remains very common: "If you make this product for your kids, they'll think you're a better mom, and you'll be the most popular mom in the neighborhood!" But what motivates women is not so much aspiration as empathy. They want to feel "warmer" toward others by finding points of commonality.

State Farm insurance has a great ad campaign that says, in effect, "We live where you live. We are like you." One particular ad features the headline "We never met a mom who wasn't working." It shows a woman getting ready for work in the morning. She's on her cell phone. She has a briefcase to keep track of. She's trying to get a shoe on one child, while another child is escaping out the door behind her. It's a scene that resonates with many, many women: "Oh, yeah. She's like me."

Men think "winner."
Women think "warmer."

Multi-tasking is a

Tell stories. Day in and day out—from telling anecdotes to sharing their "life story"—women connect through narrative. Incorporate that approach into your marketing materials.

Neiman Marcus did precisely that in its 2004 Christmas catalog, building the entire piece around stories about a handful of fictional but realistic families. Products appeared not against a plain background but within the context of one or another family's lifestyle. And there were little stories that wove the products into the lives of Mom, Dad, and the kids: Jim is nuts about snowboarding, and here's why he wants this snowboard for Christmas. Or, Mom got Jim this sweater to wear when he went skiing in Colorado.

Reach Her "While She's Here"

Multi-tasking is a way of life for women, both by inclination and by necessity. So tap into that quality by finding ways to sell them multiple things simultaneously. Unlike men, who

way of life for women.

resist calls to focus on more than one thing at a time, women are open to various "while you're here" marketing efforts—cross-selling, up-selling, and so on. They will pay attention to in-store displays and demos that encourage them to get the

---

TOM SAYS ...

HAWKISH ON DOVE

September 2004. I read two articles that converge on a single point: When it comes to reaching women, advertisers (mostly) don't know what they're doing—except when they (ever-so-occasionally) do.

(1) The *Independent* of London quotes Rebekka Bay, organizer of a Rethink Pink conference, on the subject of "advertisers' interpretation of 21st-century woman." Specifically, she argues, they cling to such unrealistic images as the "Perfect Mum," the "Alpha Female," the "Fashionista," the "Beauty Bunny," and the "Great Granny."

(2) The *Financial Times* reports: "Unilever brand Dove's use of six generously proportioned 'real women' to promote its skin-firming preparations must qualify as one of the most talked-about marketing decisions taken this summer. It was also one of the most successful: since the campaign broke, sales of the firming lotion have gone up 700 percent in the UK, 300 percent in Germany and 220 percent in the Netherlands."

Yes! (Can we see more of that, please?)

It's a stroke of genius.

most out of their time in your store. The logic is simple, and to women it's compelling: "While you're here, why don't you try this new product? While you're here, as long as you're buying a jar of jelly, we'll give you a price break on peanut butter. You don't need peanut butter this week, but you will need it eventually."

TOM SAYS ...

FLICK CHICK TICKED
Marti is right: People Power sells. But Madison Avenue is slow to "get it." And so is … Hollywood.

A couple of years ago, a senior Hollywood producer

(a woman) told me this: "Each time a 'women's movie' is a success—like *The First Wives Club*— everybody in the industry is surprised all over again, and nothing much

happens. But if some 'action movie' is a hit, it instantly spawns a dozen frenzied knock-offs."

Egads!

Some retailers are already doing a lot in this area. H-E-B, one of the leading grocery chains in the southwest, has developed a store-within-a-store approach that brings companies like Payless Shoe Source, Wells Fargo bank, and Verizon Wireless literally under the H-E-B roof. It's a very savvy strategy: Women get more done, they buy more stuff, H-E-B garners more customers—everybody's happy.

A related concept is intercept marketing. At one point, Toyota had one of its new cars parked near Pier 39, a big tourist center in San Francisco. Sightseers and other passers-by could easily stop to check out the vehicle. They could also enter their name in a contest to win a new Toyota of their own. To be sure, men love cars, and some men did check out this car. But women—because of their "on the way" mentality, because they are eager to maximize their experience—are more apt to digress from their appointed mission in order to explore some new opportunity.

Intercept marketing: Go where women are, and "head them off at the pass." They'll be glad you did.

Design with Women in Mind

Women perceive a finer level of detail than men, and they harbor a longer list of wants than men. So one very promising way to grab them is by excelling at the practical and aesthetic nuances of design.

Consider product design. With computers and consumer electronics, for example, innovation efforts tend to focus on technical features: faster processing speed, bigger memory, speakers that boom more loudly. But what about creating systems of devices that (a) look good in their own right, as objects of home décor, and (b) go together as a set? Why, for most computers and televisions and stereo components, are choices limited to either a silver box or a black box? The manufacturer that recognizes how much those considerations matter to women will reap a windfall.

The makers of one product, Dutch Boy Paint, have shown how a simple, women-friendly design change can work wonders. Dutch Boy redesigned its paint can to be less messy, easier to carry, and easier to store. It's a stroke of genius.

trends

&

it's not rocket science

Another huge area of opportunity involves retail design. Several points come to mind:

Environmental "clean-up." In all of the five senses except that of sight, women have greater sensitivity than men. Which means that your store environment has a big impact on them, for good or ill. If it's a little dirty, if it's a little disorganized, if it doesn't smell quite right, women will avoid it. Automotive service outlets, for example, often fail this test. Conversely, one excellent way to attract women is by designing your place so that it appeals to the senses. Mrs. Fields cookie shops and other bakeries do well in this regard.

Outfit merchandising. Organize goods not just according to category, but also according to context. Home-improvement stores are starting to go this route. Instead of just putting bathtubs here and sinks over there and toilets over in some other place, they are presenting these items as collections or suites of products. Plus, you might see a collection accessorized with a Kleenex holder, a toothbrush cup, towels, and so forth.

Family-friendly convenience. Make it easy for women with young kids in tow to navigate your store. Provide suitable shopping carts, make your aisles wide, and maintain safe, clean, usable restrooms. Those amenities will encourage harried moms to stay in your store longer.

TOM SAYS ...

RESTROOM BREAK

A few years ago, I had the distinct honor of keynoting the convention of the American Institute of Architects. And I had the distinct pleasure of giving my audience hell about ... the Women's Issue.

Did I talk about the Glass Ceiling? No! I talked about ... the Women's Room. I made my point by outlining a simple exercise to my (mostly) male audience.

Instructions:

1. Purchase ticket to the symphony (7:30 p.m. show).

2. Drink three large bottles of water between 5 p.m. and 7 p.m.

3. Cross-dress.

4. At Intermission, wait in line at the women's restroom.

5. Squirm.

6. Keep squirming.

7. Realize that you, Mr. Male Architect, are a total wretch.

8. Return to the auditorium, seize the microphone, and apologize ... publicly ... to every woman in the hall.

Try it yourself. Go to a symphony, a play, a ballet—whatever. Note what happens during Intermission.

Men's room: no line, no problem!

Women's room: lines that seem to stretch for half a block.

Will "we" ever learn?

Somehow ... I fear not.

Allow for physical differences.

&

Help women work through their
"longer list."

Allowing for physical differences. Women, on average, are shorter and have less upper-body strength than men. Keep that fact in mind when arranging products in your store—especially if you're a home-improvement company or one of those big-box retailers that stack merchandise to the rafters.

Prepare to Compare:
Finding "the Perfect Answer"

Quite simply, a woman will not buy the first thing she finds that meets her top criteria. She will not make a purchase until she has looked at a full range of options—until she has done what she considers to be due diligence on that decision. Make that tendency work in your favor. Be a source of ample and useful information about products or services in your industry.

Your Web site is a great place to help women work through their "longer list." So use up-to-date digital tools to let women drill down for data as far as they want. Facilitate comparisons, both within your own product portfolio and with competitors' products.

For example, if you're presenting investment information to a woman investor, don't present just one option. Present two or three options: "Here's one at the high-risk end of the range, here's one at the low-risk end, and here's one in the middle. And here are the pros and cons of each option."

Sometimes, with their drive for the "perfect answer," women get in their own way. They never know when they have found and considered all available options. (Yes, once in a while, we'll admit that.) So part of your job as a marketer is to help them break through that decision reluctance.

Mazda, in some of its showrooms, includes kiosks that allow shoppers to compare Mazda models with other manufacturers' models. By facilitating her ability to conduct a comparison right there in the showroom, Mazda helps her move through the decision process more swiftly. And, to a small but significant extent, these kiosks let Mazda control the competitive research that she is going to do anyway. The company must be honest about the comparison that it provides, but it does get to make sure that Mazda's virtues get full coverage.

trends & it's not rocket science

TOM SAYS ...

"ROARING" SUCCESS (II): INVESTING IN WOMEN

People regularly ask me, Where are the examples of companies that take the women's market seriously? For a long, long time, the answer was clear: There aren't any. But over the past few years, some companies have begun to catch on. A brief survey:

Jiffy Lube. *Faith Popcorn, in her book* EVEolution *(co-authored with Lys Marigold), presents Jiffy Lube as one of her favorite case studies: "In the male mold, Jiffy Lube was going all-out to deliver quick, efficient service. But, in the female mold, women were being turned off by the 'let's get it fixed fast, no conversation required' experience." The new Jiffy Lube is working to change all that. The premise of the change, as it affects the woman customer:* "Control *over her environment.* Comfort *in the service setting.* Trust *that her car is being serviced properly. ...* Respect *for her intelligence and ability."*

Lowe's. *From a Forbes.com article that was posted a couple of years ago: "[W]omen, according to Lowe's research, initiate 80 percent of all home-improvement decisions, especially the big-ticket orders like kitchen cabinets, flooring and bathrooms. 'We focused on a customer nobody in home improvement has focused on. Don't get me wrong, but women are far more discriminating than men,' says [CEO Robert] Tillman." What Lowe's has done to attract women: better lighting, wider aisles, cleanliness, packaging that focuses on benefits rather than on tech specs.*

Mattel. *Headline to an April 2002* Wall Street Journal *article: "Mattel Sees Untapped Market for Blocks: Little Girls." According to the piece, "Last year, more than 90 percent of LEGO sets purchased were for boys. ... Mattel says Ello—with interconnecting plastic squares, balls, triangles, squiggles, flowers and sticks, in pastel colors and with rounded corners—will go beyond LEGO's linear play patterns."*

Procter & Gamble. *Headline to a June 2002 cover story in* Advertising Age: *"Crest Spin-off Targets Women." The product: Crest Rejuvenating Effects. The leadership group: Crest's "chicks in charge" team. The nitty-gritty: a $50 million advertising campaign, new packaging, and other changes.*

Efforts in the financial-services industry have been especially encouraging. (As Marti notes, banks and brokerages often lead the way—because they know where the money is!) A few years ago, a piece in the San Jose Mercury News *offered these examples:*

Citigroup. *In October 2001, "Citigroup rolled out Women & Co., a membership service aimed at women under 55 who have $100,000 in investable assets."*

Wells Fargo. *In June 2002, "Wells Fargo Bank earmarked an extra $5 billion for its Women's Loan Program." That's on top of $10 billion that Wells Fargo had previously committed.*

Merrill Lynch. *Merrill Lynch has set up "a multi-cultural and diversified business development group this year to target women and ethnic investors. The focus is on forums where female investors can learn and network."*

Charles Schwab. *Charles Schwab is promoting Women Investing Now, an educational initiative that "features classes taught by women."*

Cents & Sensibility. *Financial planners Erin J. Kincheloe and Sharon A. Almeida gave their practice "a face lift in mid-2000 to appeal more to women, who make up three out of every four clients," the* Mercury News *reports. "They started with a new name—Cents & Sensibility, a play on Jane Austen's novel* [Sense and Sensibility]. *Other cues run from the magazines in the lobby (the Academy Award issue of* People, *not* Forbes *or* Fortune*) to the office décor (impressionistic paintings, not historical stock-market charts). Most important, they spend more time talking with women about what they want to accomplish with their money—such as saving for college or helping family—rather than how they'll grow it. For example, their sessions for women have 'changed from a pretty analytical male-think type of seminar with all these facts, into something that starts with the heart and ends with the figures,' Kincheloe said."*

The good news: These cases actually do *exist.*

The bad news: Only one of them, that of Cents & Sensibility, involves a company that has moved strategically … to reorient its enterprise around the women's market.

But I'll take what I can get.

trends
&
it's not rocket science

Save Her Time

Want to win over the hearts of women? *Save them time.*
Women live a different lifestyle than men do. Some people
call this phenomenon "the double day." While the situation
in the workplace has changed quite a bit over the past couple
of decades, the situation at home hasn't changed quite so
fast. Yes, men are helping out more than they used to. But
on average, full-time working wives still spend twice as many
hours per week on childcare and household chores than their
full-time working husbands do.

Women are absolutely time-starved. Even women who
stay at home and care for young kids are on a tight schedule.
When the time comes to pick up your kids, the folks who
baby-sit them or who staff their daycare center will *not* wait
for you. A woman in that situation simply doesn't have five or
ten minutes to spare. If she has to leave a cart just sitting in a
retailer's aisle so that she can get to the daycare center on time,
that's what she'll do. Retailers should be more aware of those
sources of frustration and stress.

Retailers should also recognize that women often have
no choice but to shop with kids in tow. It's just not possible
for them to hire a babysitter every time they need to run an
errand. A few smart companies have reckoned with that
issue. The furniture chain IKEA, for example, now features
a playroom for kids in its stores. It also operates a little café.
Why is that important? When young kids get hungry, they
want to eat *right away*. If there isn't a place where Mom can
get them a snack, then she'll take them and leave the store.
My gym, Lifetime Fitness, also does a great job in this respect.
It has a wonderful daycare area where you can bring your
kids for up to two hours. It's safe. It's well-staffed. And you
can bet that women use that gym more often, and retain their
memberships longer, because they can drop off their kids
while they work out.

Here's a business idea that would be a big winner: Women
with new babies must deal with huge amounts of *stuff*—heavy
stuff, stuff that needs to be hauled in every week: bales of
diapers, cases of infant formula and baby food, boxes of baby-
wipes. What if some retailer (a combination of Peapod and

Women often have no choice but to shop with kids in tow.

Toys"R"Us, I suppose) found a way to deliver that stuff on a weekly schedule? Women would simply figure out how much of each staple they need each week, and then deliveries would follow automatically.

Believe me: Offering services of that kind will set you far apart from competitors and win you a very warm spot in women's hearts.

Easy Money: Get to Her First

Thus far, very few companies are even trying to appeal to women in the manner that I've outlined here. Right now, in the marketplace, there is very little competitive clutter.

That surprises me. With big-ticket categories, for example, companies have been slow to act on the data about women's role in buying decisions that Tom and I have set forth. I

trends &

it's not rocket science

would expect to see lots of ads for computers and consumer electronics in women's magazines, on women's cable channels, and in women's media in general. I don't see them. Why not?

But the absence of clutter translates into an abundance of opportunity. This is Strategy 101: *First in, first win*. So get out there. Get into the women's market before your competitor does. Align your message with female gender culture.

Marketing to women is easy money. Why do I say that?

First, marketing to women is not rocket science. It's not extraordinarily complex. Once you consider a few basic features of female gender culture, many details of execution will fall naturally into place.

Second, it requires no real increase in your marketing budget. You just need to spend your money *differently*— in a way that aligns with the priorities and preferences of your primary buyer.

Third, its impact on profitability is huge. In category after category, for small businesses and for big corporations, women are your primary buyer. Moreover, their sustained loyalty and their high propensity to make referrals give you much more bang for your marketing buck.

Fourth, as I mentioned earlier, when you market successfully to women, you increase your customer satisfaction among men as well.

Women believe in achieving a win-win solution. For you and your business, marketing to women is a win-win solution.

TOM SAYS ...

NO MORE MS. NICHE GAL

As Marti says, marketing to women isn't rocket science. But it does require real commitment. Real ... Leadership.

In the last chapter of her marvelous book *Marketing to Women*, Marti offers a few "Notes to the CEO." Herewith, a sampling of her main points. (Hey, I'm a guy. I think in headlines.)

1. Women are not a "niche." So do not consign them to a so-called "Specialty Markets" group.

2. If you "dip your toes in the water," what makes you think that you'll get splashy results?

3. Bust through the walls of the corporate silos in your company. One must bring the ... Total Enterprise ... to bear on this enormous opportunity.

4. Once you get her, don't let her slip away. Women: tough to convince, fiercely loyal once you have won them over.

5. WOMEN ARE ... THE MAIN GAME!

TOP 10 TO-DOs

1. *Ditch "niche."* Resist the temptation to paint your brand pink, or to consign women to the "specialty market" ghetto. Women aren't "special." They are a huge and eminently reachable market.

2. *Set the stage.* Analyze, and organize your marketing operation around, the entire buying process. Treat all five stages (from initial interest to the post-purchase relationship) as equally important.

3. *Start a rumor.* Tap into the power that is women's conversation. Remember: The first three letters of "women" are WOM— which spell word-of-mouth.

4. *Face forward.* Let customers see your human side. Show people (real people, not idealized models) in your communications.

5. *Warm up.* Base your messaging on an appeal to empathy rather than envy. (Again, think "warmer," not "winner.")

6. *Put it all together.* Explore the potential of outfit merchandising, experiential marketing, and other approaches that cater to women's holistic, "all under one roof" sensibility.

7. *Go "home."* Design your physical spaces to make women feel comfortably at home. Key points: cleanliness, convenience, kids.

8. *Dare to compare.* Be forthright about how your products and services stack up against those of your competitors. Women will make that comparison anyway, so why not help them out?

9. *Take note.* Learn from examples (such as those listed by Tom) of companies that are beginning to hear "women roar." Study those cases, steal from them, improve on them.

10. *Get a jump.* Act now. Survey the virtually wide-open territory that the women's market represents—and be among the first to venture into it. ("First in, first win," remember?)

4

Maturity Mania:
Where the Money Is (II)

Contrasts

Was	Is
Gray means "gray"	Gray means *green*
Retirement	Rejuvenation
"Borrowed time"	"Decades to go"
Old = Decrepit	Old = Active
Marketing mantra: "18 to 44"	Marketing mantra: "50 and up"
"Older people don't switch brands"	"Older people do *make* brands"
Fountain of "youth"	Freedom of "age"
"Running out the clock"	"Revving up the engine"
"I am now starting to clip coupons"	"I have not yet begun to spend!"

!Rant

We are not prepared ...

We remain **CAUGHT IN THE GRIP OF A "YOUTH FETISH."** • We orient most of our enterprise activity ... in marketing, in product development, even in strategy ... **toward the over-coveted 18-44-year-old demographic set.** • We assume, wrongly, that older consumers **CONSTITUTE A STAGNANT, UNAPPROACHABLE MARKET** ... and thus we overlook an ENORMOUS OPPORTUNITY. • **But we must understand that the 50-plus population is growing immensely—both in terms of numbers and in terms of wealth.** • And to serve that market we must ... *completely reorient our enterprises.*

!Vision

I imagine ...

A STREAM OF NEW PRODUCTS DESIGNED FOR OLDER CONSUMERS who seek not to "give in to" the aging process ... but to confront and transcend it.

The development of new marketing approaches by people who don't worship at the Altar of Youth ... approaches to marketing that recognize the particular demands and **ABUNDANT WEALTH** of Boomers, who are used to ... Getting Their Own Way.

AN UNDERSTANDING by business leaders of all stripes that **Boomers and other Mature consumers are *not* just a "niche" or a "segment."** • They are a **GIGANTIC VAULT:** one of the few "places" (along with the Women's Market) ... Where the Money Is ... today.

"Meat Market" Madness

Several years ago, I had the privilege of speaking to the International Health, Racquet & Sportsclub Association (IHRSA) in San Francisco.

A bit of background: I've been fighting weight problems since I was a kid. Quite recently I've had a fair bit of success in that fight. But at the time of this speaking gig, my success on that front had been (shall we say) rather modest. And there I was, addressing a group of several thousand health-club owners and managers. So lean. So fit. So vibrant. And: So annoying! (Not a male waist bigger than 32 inches ... or so I imagined.)

**Love Me!
LOVE MY
WALLET!**

The moment came in my remarks to IHRSA members when I harangued them about the biggest trend that their industry confronts. I unveiled a slew of startling statistics (statistics that came from IHRSA, of all places) on the demographic tidal wave bearing down on them. Then the show's lighting director—I had connived with him beforehand—put the spotlight on my none-too-emaciated frame. And I bellowed:

"BEHOLD ... the Body of Your Future!

"Love me! Love my ... Wallet!"

Some attendees laughed. Some scowled. No matter.

I WAS RIGHT.

Health- and sports-club types love to serve people with young, trim bodies. And yet, it is people like me—the not-so-young and not-so-trim, but ever-so-determined and ever-so-flush-

MEMBERSHIP DOOZY

IHRSA sent me a bale of background material. I was surprised ... no, STUNNED ... by one set of stats in particular.

Between 1987 and 1997, IHRSA-club membership among those aged 18 to 34 grew by 27 percent. Among those aged 35 to 54, membership grew by 103 percent. And what about those aged 55 and above? Membership growth: 123 percent.

Between 1987 and 2002, IHRSA-club membership among the 55-plus set grew by ... 265 percent!

Talk about bulking up!

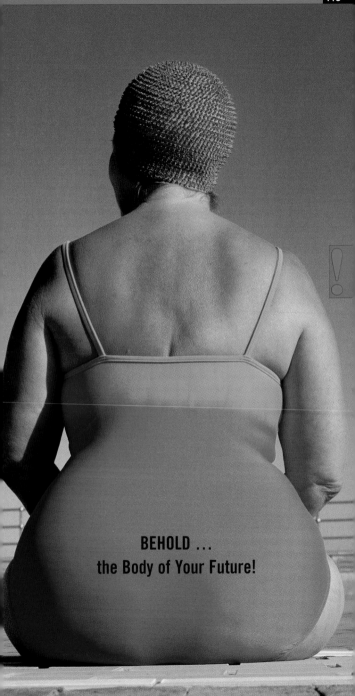

BEHOLD ...
the Body of Your Future!

REJECT:
"IT'S 18–44, STUPID!"

EMBRACE:
"18–44 IS STUPID, STUPID!"

with-disposable-income—who embody the real growth market for their historically youth-obsessed business.

Despite my advanced age, I am more than willing (make that delighted!) to look at attractive members of the opposite sex. Nonetheless, I would rather not work out ... in my bumbling, puffing fashion ... in an atmosphere geared toward Human Machines.

Health clubs are not designed for, or marketed to, people like me.

Why not?

Don't they like money?

Marketing Mantra Makeover

America loves youth! More to the point: Marketing types love youth!

Implicitly if not explicitly, marketers develop and direct almost every product or service you can imagine ... around the goal of attracting the attention of teens and young adults, and keeping those consumers as "customers for life."

Hence the marketing mantra (and I mean *the* Marketing Mantra): "It's 18–44, Stupid!"

What a load of crap!

I have a suggestion. No ... a COMMAND.

Reject: "It's 18–44, Stupid!"

Embrace: "18–44 Is Stupid, Stupid!"

We are getting older. LOTS OF US. The populations of industrialized nations are aging. FAST. And the meaning of "older" and "aging" is changing. RADICALLY.

trends

maturity mania

GRAY EXPECTATIONS
Compared with other fully developed nations, the U.S. rate of aging is far from extreme. Indeed, the Aging Thing... and its manifold implications ... will be much *more extreme* in Western Europe and Japan than in the United States.

Italy, for instance, recently passed a first-time-in-human-history threshold: There are more Italians over 60 years of age than there are Italians under age 20.

Overall in the industrialized countries, the over-60 crowd makes up 20 percent of the population, up from 12 percent in 1950. And they are on the way to forming *one-third* of the population by 2050. (In Japan, that figure will be a staggering *40 percent!*)

An overview of my argument in this chapter:

1. The "new mature" are numerous.
2. They are astonishingly wealthy.
3. They have *decades* of free-spending years left.
4. They are accustomed to being well served by commercial enterprise.
5. They are now being ill served by commercial enterprise. (The older they get, it seems, the more steadfastly enterprise seeks to *avoid* their custom.)

This trend is big. So must be our response to it.

Do the Math: Attack of the Godzilla Geezer

It stalks the land, threatening to ravage and transform the business landscape. What is "it"? A demographic behemoth that I call … the Godzilla Geezer. "Geezer" may not be quite the right term for so energetic a creature. But calling it Godzilla is *exactly* right: The "new old" are trouncing through the marketplace with … unstoppable force.

If you remember nothing else from this chapter, please remember the following set of simple stats. In the United States, between 2002 and 2010 …

The number of people between 18 and 44 years of age (remember the overweaning 18–44 mantra) will DECLINE by 1 percent.

(DECLINE = -1%.)

The number of people who are 55 years of age and older will INCREASE by 21 percent.

(INCREASE = +21%.)

The number of people between 55 and 64 years of age will increase by … 47 percent.

(INCREASE = +47%.)

The only proper response to numbers like these: Holy smoke!

MEDIAN COOL

David B. Wolfe, author of Ageless Marketing: Strategies for Reaching the Hearts and Minds of the New Customer Majority, *reports that in the United States the median adult age is now 45. (And, again, that number will keep going up.) So, demographically speaking, marketers with an 18–44 fixation are looking in completely the wrong direction.*

See also the Cool Friend interview with Wolfe, page 134.

Do the Math: Codgers with Cash

As with the "Women Roar" Thing, so with the "Maturity Mania" Thing: Businesses are neglecting a market that is HUGE, not only in terms of population trends ... but also in terms of ... Where the Loot Is. As a group, people in their fifties and older are reaching their peak earning power, and have amassed incredible assets.

As of 2001, Americans aged 50 and older held *$29.1 trillion* in net worth. That amounted to *69 percent* of the total net worth held in the United States. It also represents a 56 percent jump in the amount held by this age group in 1983.

There's more. According to data gathered by the U.S. Census Bureau and by the Federal Reserve, households headed by someone aged 55 to 64 had a median net worth in 2000 of about $112,000 ... that is, *15 times* as much as the median net worth (about $7,200) of the under-35 age group.

trends

maturity mania

HEY: BIG SPENDERS!

Carol Morgan and Doran Levy, in their marvelous book *Marketing to the Mindset of Boomers and Their Elders*, offer stunning statistics on the economic power that mature consumers—Boomers and others—represent.

They choose age 40 as their threshold for measurement. While 40 might seem young to some of you (and me), that's not what marketers think.

They shower attention on teens and twenty-somethings—and pay almost as little attention to forty-somethings as they do to members of the 50-plus bunch.

Morgan and Levy write: "Households headed by someone 40 and older enjoy 91 percent [or *$9.7 trillion*] of our population's net worth."

And: "The mature market is the dominant market in the U.S.

economy, making the majority of expenditures in virtually every category."

Please reread that last sentence. Slowly. Then share it with a colleague. Or two or three. (Or 23.) Key words: EVERY. CATEGORY.

Ken Dychtwald, author of *Age Power: How the 21st Century Will Be Ruled by the New Old*, has been covering the mature market for more than two decades. Here are some figures that he adduces regarding the buying power of consumers in the 50-plus market:

- They (79 percent of them, to be precise) overwhelmingly own their own homes.
- There are 40 million credit-card users among them.
- They buy 41 percent of new cars and 48 percent of all luxury cars.
- They account for $610 billion in healthcare spending, and for 74 percent of prescription-drug spending.

Which leads Dychtwald to wonder: *Why are they the target of only 5 percent of advertising dollars?*

Why?

The Age-Old "Old Age" Taboo

" 'Age Power' will rule the 21st century," writes Dychtwald, "and ... we are woefully unprepared."

"Woefully unprepared": I humbly disagree with that assessment. It is not that "we" are "unprepared." It is that "we" ... JUST DON'T SEEM TO GIVE A SHIT.

Strong language. But I don't see how the cold, hard facts in the matter could lead to any other conclusion.

I once asked Dychtwald why people continued to pay so little attention to such an enormous issue. His take: We are so youth-obsessed that we remain squeamish, frankly, about the very notion of getting older. Aging, indeed, is frighteningly close to ... a Taboo Subject.

"GRAY" UNDER PRESSURE?

Unlike the Women's Market, this Mature Market applies to me personally. Age-wise, I'm approaching official U.S. retirement age (65). I'm in no hurry to grow older, but I don't have any choice in the matter. So: Will somebody help me—and tens of millions like me—as we continue our "travels"? If you do, we will shower you with riches. And, actuarially speaking, we will do so for many years to come.

Remember the famous clarion call of naval commander John Paul Jones during the American Revolutionary War: "I have not yet begun to fight"?

Well ... I HAVE NOT YET BEGUN TO SPEND!

I HAVE NOT YET BEGUN TO SPEND.

Fine. Ignore it. But ignoring it won't make it go away. If you're in business today, ignoring the mature market will cause you to ignore enormous potential revenues.

To put it bluntly:

TRILLIONS UPON TRILLIONS (UPON TRILLIONS) OF DOLLARS ARE ... UP FOR GRABS. (In the United States alone.)

trends

maturity mania

GOING LIKE 60 (MILES PER HOUR)— AT 60 (YEARS OF AGE)

Not long ago, I saw a cover headline on *AARP The Magazine* that hit the "New Aging" thing with bull's-eye precision:

"Sixty Is the New Thirty."

Indeed.

AGE OF DISCRETION

In marketing, it matters not just .... Where the Money Is ... but also ... how easily you can pry it loose. The name of the game: *discretionary income.* And according to the U.S. Bureau of Labor Statistics, the percentage of household income that counts as "discretionary" is highest among the 65–74 age group.

Voices: In the Demographic Dogma House

"Advertisers pay more to reach the kid because they think that once someone hits middle age he's too set in his ways to be susceptible to advertising. ... In fact, this notion of impressionable kids and hidebound geezers is little more than a fairy tale, a Madison Avenue gloss on Hollywood's cult of youth."

—James Surowiecki, the *New Yorker*, April 2002

"Many businesses have not yet shed the outdated view that the mature market is made up of stingy old-timers set in their ways. Unless you are in the business of prescription drugs or retirement homes, the argument goes, why bother?"

—The *Economist*, August 2002

"Marketers' attempts at reaching those over 50 have been miserably unsuccessful. No market's motivations and needs are so poorly understood."

—Peter Francese, founding publisher of *American Demographics* magazine

"The mature market ... cannot be dismissed as entrenched in its brand loyalties."

—Carol Morgan and Doran Levy, *Marketing to the Mindset of Boomers and Their Elders*

Morgan and Levy add: *"Focused on assessing the market place based on lifetime value (LTV), marketers may dismiss the mature market as headed to its grave. The reality is that at 60 a person in the U.S. may enjoy 20 or 30 years of life."*

Yes!

trends

maturity mania

The Maturing of the "Mature" Market

In an important sense, the demographic and financial numbers involved in the mature market are the least of it. Or, at least, not the most of it. At the forefront of Maturity Mania is what I call … the Boomer Bonanza. And the salient truth about the Boomer Bonanza is this: It is … an *Entirely New Market*. Because Boomers are … an *Entirely New Group* of "aging" folks.

I turned 60 just a few years ago. My Dad is now dead, but I well remember when he turned 60. The future for him? No particular aspirations. His main idea (as they say in football and basketball): RUN OUT THE CLOCK.

NO MORE!

"I have a lot left to do.

In the United States, Boomers—those born between 1946 and 1964—number almost 80 million people. And those Boomers, whose first cohort turn 60 in 2006, have had a Unique Life History. They represent *the first generation in history to take full charge of their lives …* at every stage of their lives.

Their attitude—then and now, as young folks in the 1960s and as "old folks" in the 21st century—can be summed up in a few simple phrases:

"I am in charge."

"I am active."

"I have a lot left to do."

"And I can afford to do it."

And I can afford to do it."

Voices: The New "Age-Appropriate" Behavior

"From jogging to plastic surgery, from vegetarian diets to Viagra, [aging Boomers] are fighting to preserve their youth and defy the effects of gravity."
—M.W.C. Howgill, "Healthcare Consumerism, the Information Revolution, and Branding"

"The Latest Golden-Years Trend: Going Back to College."   **—Headline, *Newsweek*, June 2002**

"Such a critical mass of older women with a tradition of rebellion and independence and a way of making a living has not occurred before in history."
—Gerda Lerner, historian

"NOT ACTING THEIR AGE: As Baby Boomers Zoom into Retirement, Will America Ever Be the Same?"
—Headline, *U.S. News & World Report*, June 2001

The answer to the *U.S. News* query is implicit in the question itself: NO! Boomers are NOT "acting their age"—and they don't intend to.

And the United States (along with Western Europe, Japan, and the rest of the developed world) *will never be the same.* NEVER.

You're Only As Old As You ... Look!

"Growing old gracefully" used to mean "giving in to nature." No longer. Older folks are rewriting that old joke "Age before beauty." The new motto: "Age *and* beauty."

From a 2002 Associated Press report:

"After Hazel York's husband died, she moved into a retirement home, convinced the better part of her life was over. Then she met Damon. She's 81. He's 79. They were married about a year and a half ago at The Village Community Care Retirement Community in Hemet, Calif. She feels she won a second chance at life, so she decided to give her face a second chance, too. York underwent a five-hour face-lift in June in Beverly Hills, Calif., to erase some wrinkles and shave off a few years. Her husband is supportive, but said, 'I love her as is.' She says she did it for herself. 'Don't get me wrong. I don't want to look 16 again,' she said, 'but I also don't want to look like Damon's mother.'

"Experts say thousands of men and women 65 and older are getting plastic surgery. They want to feel young and attractive, and battle age discrimination. Since 1997, the number of cosmetic procedures for those 65 and older jumped from about nearly 121,000 to more than 425,000 last year. Seniors accounted for about 5 percent of 8.5 million surgeries performed in 2001, according to the American Society for Aesthetic Plastic Surgery in Los Alamitos, Calif.

"Dr. Sheldon Sevinor, a plastic surgeon based in Boston, said he had at least 30 patients last year that are older than 70. 'We're living longer and feeling more vital,' he said. 'Age 40 today is what age 30 used to be like.' He recently performed breast enlargement surgery on an 82-year-old Boston woman, his oldest patient to have the

trends

maturity mania

GOLDEN YEARS, GOLDEN WORDS
According to Ken Dychtwald, author of *Age Wave*, these are the key terms that define the lifestyle priorities of what he calls the "new old":
"Experiences."
"Convenience."
"Comfort."
"Access."

Everything We "Know" About Old Folks ...
Is Wrong!

procedure. 'She's healthy, she's spunky and she wanted to look how she felt,' he said. ...

"Dr. John Grossman, who performed York's surgery and runs cosmetic surgery clinics in Denver and Beverly Hills, Calif., said he has had many patients her age. 'Hazel's a perfect example that chronological age doesn't have to relate to how you feel about yourself. Just because you're 80 doesn't mean you have to look and feel like it,' he said."

GROWING ... GRACEFUL

Another quote that nicely captures what "growing old gracefully" means today: "Pick up any copy of Glamour *or* Men's Health*, and you'll see pages of advertisements encouraging readers to enlarge their breasts, retard baldness, correct their vision, improve their smile, or relieve stress through herbs, massage therapy, acupuncture—you name it."*

(That's from the book Beyond Managed Care: How Consumers and Technology Are Changing the Future of Health Care, *by Dean C. Coddington, Elizabeth A. Fischer, Keith D. Moore, and Richard L. Clarke.)*

---

trends

maturity mania

Do the Math: Aging Assumptions

Assumptions, assumptions. In business, they can kill you. Especially when it comes to understanding (and marketing to) Boomers and others in the mature market. More and more, it's becoming clear that ... Everything We "Know" About Old Folks ... Is Wrong!

Two classic marketing assumptions: We assume that as women grow older, they become less fashion-conscious. And we assume that going to the movies is a teen and twenty-something thing (hence the aggressively youth-oriented fare that Hollywood puts out).

Wrong. And wrong. Two startling stats, courtesy of Carol Morgan and Doran J. Levy:

"Women 65 and older spent $14.7 billion on apparel in 1999, almost as much as that spent by 25- to 34-year-olds. While spending by the older women increased from the previous year by 12 percent, that of the younger group increased only 0.1 percent. But who in the fashion industry is currently pursuing this market?"

(Holy smoke!)

"While the average American aged 12 and older watched at least five movies per year in a theater, those 40 and older were the most frequent moviegoers, viewing 12 or more per year."

(Holy smoke!)

"OLD" MOVIES

Hey, I loved The Royal Tenenbaums. *Watched it twice in theaters, three times in hotels. Made me aware of what's not available on the silver screen. Namely, smart, fun movies aimed at adults.*

Psst: Are you paying attention, Hollywood?

Geezer Goods: A Market Comes of Age

What would feeding the Godzilla Geezer market actually look like? What kinds of products would companies roll out if they truly caught Maturity Mania? The *Economist*, in a rare article on this topic, surveyed a few signs of promise ... signs that are glimmerings of What Might Be:

Makeup. In 2001
cosmetics maker L'Oréal signed up then-57-year-old French actress Catherine Deneuve to plug its products. Estée Lauder countered by turning to Karen Graham, a 1970s model.

Margarine.
Unilever's margarine category was slumping until it introduced Pro-activ, a spread that has the side benefit of lowering cholesterol. *Kaboom!* An entire division was rejuvenated.

Mineral water. Danone introduced
calcium-rich mineral water. Great. Better yet, it created packaging for the product that features larger print, as well as an easy-grip cap that aids arthritics.

Telephones.

NTT DoCoMo introduced a new cell phone, Raku-Raku ("easy-easy"), with larger buttons and easier-to-read numbers. (Where can I get one?) Intriguingly, but perhaps not surprisingly, younger folks loved it, too.

Transit.

Paris public transport (RATP) introduced an easy-to-read, simplified map for the aging population. Acceptance was universal, and the old map was dumped.

Cars.

From the article in the *Economist*: "To help young designers to understand older users' limitations, Age Concern, a British non-profit organisation, has developed a 'through other eyes' training programme for retailers. It tries to simulate the physical limitations that older customers experience when shopping. Ford, a car maker, has come up with something called 'the third-age suit' to help its design engineers—most of whom are under 40—grasp the needs of aging drivers. The outfit adds about 30 years to the wearer's age by stiffening the knees, elbows, ankles and wrists. It also adds material at the waist—a rotund stomach affects people's ability to sit

trends

maturity mania

easily—and it has gloves that reduce the sense of touch. Ford's lucky designers also have to wear yellow scratched goggles to find out what it is like to have cataracts. The exercise has been fruitful. Thanks to the third-age suit, the company's cars are now easier for everyone to get into and out of; their seat belts are more comfortable to wear; glare has been reduced; and the controls are more readable and reachable."

My Target: "Target" Marketing

Those are all great cases. But they are just ... *cases*. Isolated events in a ... Grand Marketing Narrative ... that continues to treat Youth as its hero.

They are a far cry from ... Strategic Realignment. And anything less than Strategic Realignment—that is, reorienting your enterprise from the ground up to serve the emerging markets—will leave you in the cramped, low-growth world of "niche" marketing.

Martha Barletta, in her book *Marketing to Women*, begs CEOs not to consign women to a "specialty market group." Women *are* the market, she insists.

The same basic argument applies ... with equal force ... to the 50-plus market.

Simply review the numbers: If a group controls the vast majority of wealth and discretionary income, then ... it *is* the market.

GET A GRIP

Serving the "older" market has knock-on effects down the age scale.

A wonderful case in point: OXO-brand kitchen devices, whose arthritic-friendly grips have made them global bestsellers among people of all ages.

"ZOOM" TIME

Headline from *Advertising Age:* "Take the Road Less Traveled." The story: Sony is belatedly targeting "Zoomers," the heretofore neglected 34 percent of its customers who are aged 50 and older.

trends

maturity mania

IF A GROUP CONTROLS THE VAST MAJORITY OF WEALTH AND DISCRETIONARY INCOME, THEN ... IT *IS* THE MARKET.

But please, do not assume that my argument here is "about" marketing. Rather: It is about marketing ... *and* product development ... *and* distribution ... *and* operations ... *and* branding ... *and* strategy. In conclusion:

Think ... BOOMERS.
Think ... "GEEZERS."
Think ... MATURITY MANIA.
Think ... TRILLIONS OF DOLLARS.
Think ... STRATEGIC REALIGNMENT.

GOING, GOING ... STRATEGIC!

It was a gorgeous, late-July morning on Martha's Vineyard. I was at breakfast at the Black Dog Café with a very senior executive from an enormous corporation.

During our conversation, I got to talking about my pet obsessions (the "Women's Thing," the "Mature Thing"): "I see lots of 'initiatives' around. Some bank launches a 'Women's Initiative.' Some health-services company starts a program to focus on Boomers. But I don't see anybody ... ANYBODY ... that is 'Going Strategic' around any of these trends.

"Tell me," I continued, almost pleading with him, "have I got it wrong?"

"No," he shot back, "you don't have it wrong."

We talked on, changed subjects a dozen times, and wandered back to the topic of what I call ... "TrendsWorthTrillions."

"I don't know why it hasn't 'gone strategic,' as you put it," he said. "I think we treat it as an aside, and that there is no real champion who holistically shoves it down our throats, day in and day out. Want to do that for us?"

I'm not looking for a full-time job. But I am looking to goad people into going beyond the "initiative" mentality.

So please ... Go Strategic!

TOP 10 TO-DOs

1. *Grow up.* Outgrow the taboo against taking mature consumers seriously. Don't be squeamish. "BEHOLD ... The body of Your Future!" More to the point: Behold the *customer* of your future.

2. *Grow "young."* Get ready for Ageless Marketing (as David Wolfe calls it). Yes, the population is "growing old." Yet the "new old" are wont to ... Think Young ... and to go beyond "age thinking" altogether.

3. *Give in.* Let Maturity Mania grab hold of you. Read the books (Ken Dychtwald, David Wolfe). Heed the stats (aging populations, asset-rich oldsters). Feed the monster (otherwise knows as ... Godzilla Geezer).

4. *Give up.* Relinquish your assumptions about "old" people. Remember: These aren't your father's (or mother's) "old folks."

5. *Talk it over.* Chat up your parents, a trusted mentor—anyone in the 50-plus set who can tell you about the Ways and Means of "mature" consumers today. Get on, now ... Listen to Your Elders!

6. *Talk it up.* Discuss Maturity Mania with your colleagues. Tell them about its (demographic) size. Sell them on its (financial) scope.

7. *Look out.* Observe the new "look" of aging—which is all about Looking Good. The age of "running out the clock" has ... run out..

8. *Look up.* Set your sights high—beyond "target" marketing, beyond "specialty" or "niche" markets. Get *manic* (in a "mature" way, of course) about Total Enterprise Realignment.

9. *Make good.* Make *goods*, that is, whose Design serves the vanities (and frailties) of 50-plus consumers. And don't be surprised if younger folks flock to buy them, too.

10. *Make money.* Cash in on the coming Boomer Bonanza. Remember that "we" (Boomers and other "mature" types) "HAVE NOT BEGUN TO SPEND." So: Have you begun to sell to us? (Why not?)

COOL FRIEND: David Wolfe

David B. Wolfe, an internationally recognized expert
in consumer behavior, focuses on what he calls the
New Customer Majority—that is, adults aged 40 and
older. His book **Serving the Ageless Market** *(1990)*
was the first business work to describe how people's
motivations and behavior change at each stage of life.
Below are remarks that he made in connection with his
most recent book, **Ageless Marketing: Strategies for**
Reaching the Hearts and Minds of the New Customer
Majority *(co-authored with Robert Snyder, 2003).*

* *

Everything we learned in marketing was pretty much
learned when youth ruled the markets. Today that is
not true. The median adult age is now 45. That means
that people in midlife and older are the New Customer
Majority, and their world views, needs, values ... are
quite different from those of the people who set the rules
before the last decade started. Twenty-five-year-olds and
45- or 55-year-olds are in different places.

* *

[L]ook at what's happened in marketing over the last
several decades. ...

In the 1980s the whole nature of the advertising
business underwent an epochal change. It started
with the Saatchi brothers, when they started acquiring
agencies. They started growing agencies through
acquisition and merger rather than through client
development. This changed the focus of agency
leadership toward business development and financial
matters. ... [Hence] by default, the creative output often
falls to the youngest people in the agency. ...

The average age of account executives, for example,
... is 28. So you've got much less experienced people,
people who are much less intuitively competent, than ...
people who once ran agencies. And what do people relate

to most? They relate to their own daily experiences. Now a 28-year-old looking at life doesn't really understand or grasp the differences between him or herself and, say, a 48-year-old.

* *

Ageless marketing is marketing that is not fundamentally rooted in a target market's age. Rather, it is rooted in the target market's value system. ...

Obviously, age comes into play. Let me give you an example. New Balance, which is an exemplar of ageless marketing, is not unmindful of age, but its central message, its brand persona, is ageless. It's ... institutional advertising and its marketing is ageless. It's very value-sensitive.

When New Balance gets into media placement or involved with its channel management, then it becomes very age-sensitive. But the whole customer universe doesn't see this. If you go into a Foot Locker, you will see a different inventory of New Balance products than if you go into Nordstrom. That's because patrons of Foot Locker are younger than those of Nordstrom. So New Balance is sensitive to age, but its central, overall theming is ageless.

* *

New Balance really addresses the needs of the inner self, where Nike addresses the needs of the outer directed self. Nike is about winning. New Balance is about being. Nike is about the smell of sweat, whereas New Balance is about the smell of nature. New Balance has an ad that shows a guy running up the mountainside overlooking this pristine sea. The headline is "The shortest distance between two points is not the point." ...

Having interviewed [New Balance Chairman and CEO] Jim Davis, I think he's not unmindful of the 800-pound gorilla out there called Nike, but in the late 1980s he started realizing that New Balance's sales to youth had fallen off. Of course a major reason was that youth was shrinking. He picked up on this, while Nike, Reebok, and Adidas didn't. People get used to a pattern, and they want to stay in that pattern. Plus, these other companies have to play to Wall Street, where New Balance, being a privately owned company, doesn't have to. So he was able to go into these older markets without any challenging from financial analysts or anybody else. And it turned out to be an extraordinarily winning decision.

* *

Chico's is a publicly traded women's retailer. Same-store sales grew at a rate of 20 percent last year. It's extraordinary. Chico's is nominally aimed at the 30-to-50 demo. But if you go into Chico's, you will see women of all ages, except maybe teens [and] young twenty-somethings. But you'll see sixty-somethings, seventy-somethings. And women love Chico's because, first of all, Chico's invented its own size. It's size 1, 2, 3. ...

And that's another facet of ageless marketing. You blur distinctions. We have been so fixed on market segmentation since Wendell Smith wrote his seminal paper on that [subject] in 1956 that we think segmentation is everything.

[S]egmentation by definition is a process of exclusion. What Chico's does with its new size category (1, 2, 3)—[well] it includes everybody.

* *

[B]oomer women are not really materially different from their mothers at the same age in terms of their basic needs. And in terms of their basic behavior. Carl Jung, many decades ago, talked about women entering midlife and becoming more masculine in their behavior. More assertive, more self-confident, higher self-esteem. And that's what boomer women are reflecting. Marketers are used to a much more submissive kind of woman, but that is not in the nature of the people who now occupy the ranks of the New Customer Majority. It never has been true of middle-aged and older women, but since in the past they were in the minority, these behaviors were not as pronounced or as visible as they now are.

* *

There was an article in the *New York Times*, in the Sunday Style section, titled "Sex Doesn't Sell: Miss Prim Is In." The article talked about how consumers are fed up with the blatant exposure of belly buttons. My wife read this article and then passed it on to me, and said, you know, "Once again they missed it." There's a change in the cultural ethos that is being driven by the emergence of the New Customer Majority.

Older people have tended always to be more conservative in their sexual mores and values than younger people. That's not new. But now that older people are the majority, it's having an influence on that aspect of the cultural ethos.

* *

[R]eliance on the numbers has really been the Achilles' heel of marketing. The fact that you can get an MBA in marketing without a single course in behavior indicates the extent of the reliance on looking at markets through numbers rather than through behavior. And that worked better when markets were younger, because younger people tend to move in tandem. If you know what the group is doing or will do, you have a pretty good idea of what the individual will do.

* *

[T]he first half of life [is] strongly focused on social actualization. And in the second half of life we begin to make the shift toward focus on self-actualization. In the first half of life, who we are is shaped, influenced, even compromised by our need to make social statements, the need to achieve a position in the social groups we are a part of. In self-actualization we begin to become more who we are fundamentally—who we are intrinsically, with less influence from the external world, from other people. We become more autonomous. We become more introspective. We become more individuated. This is part of self-actualization. And we become more focused on the real versus the charade. In the second half of life, authenticity becomes more important to us.

5

A Convergence of Opportunity: PrimeTime Women

By Martha Barletta

Contrasts

Was	Is
Men, ages 18 to 44	Women, ages 50 and up
Minivan	Convertible
Baby Boomers: youth in revolt	Baby Boomers: maturity in control
Marketers' focus: household income	Marketers' focus: accumulated assets
Penny-pinching crone	Big-spending matriarch
Hormonal (and attitudinal) divergence	Hormonal (and attitudinal) convergence
Celebrity endorsements	Real connections
Company image ideal: "hot" brand	Company image ideal: corporate halo
Satisfaction, here and now	Legacy, now and forever
Young man in a ... baseball cap	Mature woman in a ... big red hat
Soccer moms	PrimeTime Women!

!Rant

We are not prepared ...

WE REMAIN MIRED in an 18–44 mind-set—and, what's worse, **in an 18–44 male mind-set.** • The conventional wisdom of marketing has long dictated that younger men are the **MOST "HIGHLY COVETED" SEGMENT** of the population. • Yet the **big demographic, financial, and attitudinal trends of today** lead in another direction entirely. In fact, they converge on women aged 50 and older.
• **REACH THESE PRIMETIME WOMEN, AND YOU REACH A "HIDDEN" TAPROOT OF PROFITABILITY.** • Hence, the new marketer's mandate: We must reconfigure our understanding of what motivates women in general, mature consumers in general, and these **"sweet spot" women** in particular.

!Vision

I imagine ...

A **NEW SCHOOL OF ADVERTISING** that reinvents its notion of beauty to encompass **real women of all ages**—and replaces Barbie-like models with **believable women of all shapes and sizes.**

The emergence of entire new industries and product lines that serve the **ASPIRATIONS OF MATURE WOMEN** (and men)—the aspiration to develop one's real self, the aspiration to build a **legacy of connection with others** even as one remains strong and independent.

A MOVEMENT by Fortune 500 companies to staff their boards of directors with PrimeTime Women— **women of high accomplishment, women who know the market backward and forward (because, increasingly, they and other women like them *are* the market).**

Driving the Wrong Way: The Missing Market Intersection

The automotive industry. I'm sorry to keep picking on it, but it's hugely important, and its marketing miscues are hugely apparent. In Chapter 3, I noted how the folks who sell cars are almost literally blind to women's buying power in this area. And, to take up Tom's theme in Chapter 4, carmakers are very far from catching Maturity Mania. Instead, you hear them worrying about "age creep" in their market: "Oh my god! Our average customer is 49 years old. We must become more youth-oriented."

Even when they do think of women consumers, and even when they think beyond the 18–44 age segment, auto companies remain mired in stale assumptions. If they think at all of women in the mature market, for example, they think of Baby Boomer moms carting kids to soccer games. Thus, since the sport utility vehicle (SUV) has been a big growth category for 10 or 15 years, carmakers assume that it will continue to be a big growth category.

Here's what they don't see: Yesterday's "soccer mom" is today's (and tomorrow's) PrimeTime Woman.

PrimeTime Women lie at the golden intersection of the two markets that Tom and I have discussed earlier in this book. They are women in the 50-plus age group, and they represent a market force never before seen in history.

I am one of them, so I know a thing or two about how they are beginning to operate in the marketplace. Their message to automotive companies, in so many words: "SUV? Forget it. My next car says 'Not Available for Carpool.' Now it's time for a Lexus. Or maybe a convertible."

Marketers in all industries harbor the same woefully outdated bias against both women and 50-plus consumers. In each case, the story that gets told is what I call "the poor story." And in both cases, as Tom and I have demonstrated, that story is a myth. With older women, the myth gets compounded: "Oh, those poor things!" Visions of old widows pinching their pennies continue to clutter the business mind.

The language that people use doesn't help. Saying, "Our primary market opportunity is middle-aged women," for

Yesterday's "soccer mom" is
today's (and tomorrow's) PrimeTime Woman.

... the happiest stage

example, won't get you very far. (A reporter once asked me to comment on "middle-aged women," and my immediate response was "Eww!" And I *know* better.) Or consider the term "empty nester." It carries a very specific connotation: "Oh, those poor, sad women!" (There's that word again. "Poor"!) "Their children have left home. They don't know what to do with themselves. They've finished raising their families, and women are all about family, right?"

Yes, women are "all about family." (See Chapter 2.) But as they reach their fifties, the range of their interests and appetites expands—along with the range and depth of their resources.

Hence the term PrimeTime Women.

Why "PrimeTime"? Because, despite what many people think (including many who are nearing the age-50 mark), research shows that most people in their fifties and sixties find that period to be the happiest stage of their entire lives. That goes for women in particular. To be sure, they're sad to see their kids go away to college—yet they also feel liberated.

TOM SAYS ...

NOT-SO-"GRAY" EXPECTATIONS?
Gail Sheehy, writing in the July/August 2004 of *More* magazine: "For today's emancipated, educated, high-expectation women, the mid-forties to mid-fifties is the Age of Mastery."

And consider this summary heading, used in connection with *Ageless Marketing*, by David Wolfe and co-author Robert Snyder (a book that Marti and I both rely on ... and recommend wholeheartedly): "Baby-boomer Women: The Sweetest of Sweet Spots for Marketers."

And yet 9 of 10 "big" marketers don't get it. They may pay lip service to the concept, but they are light years away from responding to this stupendous opportunity.

Marti is on to something (BIG) with her vision of PrimeTime Women as the ultimate ... Convergence of Opportunity. This chapter amounts to an initial foray by her into the subject of her next book. Watch for that book. Read it when it appears. And start now to "make time" for this ... PrimeTime market.

of their entire lives ...

They have more time, more discretionary income, and more freedom to base decisions on their own needs and wants, as well as those of their families.

So when will companies begin to steer in their direction?

Demographic Destiny: It's About (Prime) Time

As a pioneer in the field of marketing to women, I occasionally field requests from companies that want me to speak to their "niche marketing group" or their "specialty marketing group." I usually say, "I'll come and talk to you. But 51 percent of the population is not a 'niche.' It's the *majority*."

The same principle applies, in essence, to the 50-plus group. In 2000, that segment accounted for 37 percent of the adult U.S. population. That's a pretty big "niche." And by 2010, its share of the adult population will be 43 percent. Here's another way to look at this trend, one that makes the point even starker: Between 1992 and 2020, the 50-plus population will increase in size by 76 percent, while the number of Americans under age 50 will actually *decrease* slightly.

Take the intersection of those two "niches" (50-plus women), and you have a population that encompasses 20 percent of all American adults. Again, some "niche"! And it's a growing niche at that. As any population becomes older, it becomes more female—for the simple reason that, on average, women's life spans are longer than those of men. Consider these current figures: At age 55, there are 116 women for every 100 men. At age 75, there are *175 women* for every 100 men. Plus, as the large cohort of Baby Boom women reach age 50 (and become PrimeTime Women!), 50-plus women's share of the population will become proportionally larger.

trends & primetime women

In marketing circles, people often target the African-American market or the Hispanic market. Rightly so. African-Americans make up roughly 10 percent of the U.S. population; Hispanics, roughly 14 percent. Those are significant segments, and there are specific ways to reach them. But compare those markets with the women's market (51 percent) and the 50-plus market (37 percent of the adult population, or 27 percent of the total population). It's not even close!

As Tom says (paraphrasing the bank robber Willie Sutton), go where the money is! The women's market and the 50-plus market are where companies will make money—big money—in the next couple of decades. More to the point, go where other marketers *aren't* going. Companies are targeting the African-American and Hispanic markets. Yet they are leaving these mega-markets largely untouched.

And they are ignoring, in particular, PrimeTime women—who are 20 percent of the adult population, 15 percent of the total population, and a huge source of practically hidden buying power.

Do the Math: Don't Think "Niche"— Think "Rich"

In previous chapters, Tom laid bare the true financial clout of women (see Chapter 1) and 50-plus consumers (see Chapter 4). Here let me reinforce just a few points.

First, regarding women, their earning or spending ability will only go up—dramatically up. In the United States (and elsewhere in the developed world), we have segued from a manufacturing economy to a service economy to an information economy. An information economy depends on a steady supply of educated talent. And for a good ten years now, women have been bringing home a healthy majority of university degrees (57 percent of bachelor's degrees, 58 percent of master's degrees, 50 percent of law degrees). Meanwhile, a labor shortage will arrive as the relatively small so-called Gen-X cohort enters the labor force as the Baby Boom cohort leaves it. The worse that labor shortage becomes, the greater the demand will be for educated women—and the more they will benefit financially as a result.

Already, asset accumulation among women is significant. They control 51 percent of all personal wealth in the United States. As noted earlier, they constitute 43 percent of all U.S. individuals with portfolios worth $500,000 or more. And that figure is moving in a direction that favors women. Between 1996 and 1998, for example, the number of women with assets of more than $500,000 grew by 68 percent, compared with a growth rate of only 35 percent among men.

Again, women's role in the buying process, at both the business and household levels, is overwhelming in its scope. Women fill the ranks of buyers and purchasing agents throughout the corporate world. They call the shots as the owners of 40 percent of U.S. small businesses. (Indeed, women—especially PrimeTime women who say "I have had it" with big business—are responsible for starting 70 percent of all new businesses.) And in the home, they are the decision makers in 80 percent of all spending.

Regarding the mature market, a key factor is the way that common terms of reference mask the buying power of 50-plus consumers. Two words tell the tale: household income. That is the statistic on which marketers usually focus.

First, 50-plus households tend not to have a lot of *income*. Reason: Members of such households are often retired; they

trends

&

primetime women

TOM SAYS ...

REALITY CHECK IN AISLE 9

To reach PrimeTime women, you need to put them in "prime" spots within your organization. Does that sound like "quotas"? Too bad. That's the reality.

Early in 2005, Marti sent me a report on which companies rank highest in the number of women that they place on their Boards of Directors. Top honors go to Albertsons, the Boise, Idaho–based grocery chain. It is the only Big Company whose board is more than 50 percent female. Actual count: 6 women out of 11 directors. (Among U.S. companies, by the way, next on the list is Wells Fargo, with a board that is 35.7 percent women.)

Here's CEO Larry Johnston, as quoted in the *Idaho Statesman*: "Women have insight into our customers that no man—no matter how bright, no matter how hard-working—can match. That's important when 85 percent of all consumer buying decisions made in our stores are made by women."

Retail analyst Burt Flickinger says that the company's "tragic flaw" had been its earlier absence of women in such top slots: "It was a bunch of old white guys making erroneous assumptions and erroneous conclusions about women and the multi-cultural consumers that make up the majority of Albertsons' customers."

All this still doesn't make it a cakewalk to go toe-to-toe against Wal*Mart in the grocery business, but it helps!

live not on salary or wage income, but on saved assets. And the people in this segment own 77 percent of U.S. financial assets. So income is essentially beside the point.

Second, a *household* consisting of 50-plus people usually has just two people in it. A younger household, with kids in it, will thus be larger. It may have a larger total income than the average older household, but that disguises the crucial difference in per-person spending. That difference is striking: Older consumers spend two and a half times as much per capita as the average American spends!

PrimeTime Power: Converging on Wealth

Women aged 50 and older are perfectly poised to gain from both of these larger trends.

Here's why: Over the next 10 to 20 years, the largest intergenerational transfer of wealth in history will take place as Baby Boomers inherit assets from their high-saving parents. And over the following 10 and 20 years, Baby Boom women will in turn inherit a vast amount of wealth from their husbands. Again, on average, women live longer than men. In the United States, for example, the average age at which women become widows is 67. The lifespan difference between men and women is only 7 years, but because women still tend to marry men who are several years older than they are, they outlive their husbands by an even larger margin— by 15 to 18 years, on average.

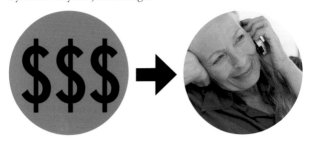

So, beginning a decade from now, women Baby Boomers will see the combined assets of both sides of their family funnel right into their wallets, and they will be in sole control of those assets for 15 to 18 years.

Already, Baby Boom women have grown accustomed to a significant role in financial activity that affects them. According to a 2004 survey cited in a Prudential Financial study, women Baby Boomers overwhelmingly report having sole or joint responsibility for managing household financial instruments such as savings accounts, investment accounts, IRAs, 401Ks, annuities, life and long-term care insurance policies, and estate plans, wills, and trusts. On average, across all of those categories, *91 percent* of Baby Boom women enjoy such responsibility, and 48 percent of them claim *sole* responsibility!

To be sure, not all Baby Boomers fall into the 50-plus category. Not yet, that is. But the ultimate power of the PrimeTime Women's market lies in the way that Baby Boom women will transform the 50-plus demographic in the coming years. Each year a new cohort of women—women who have thrived in the workplace, who have earned substantial income on their own—reaches PrimeTime age, bringing with them not only ample resources, but also the habits and expectations of financial power.

Every time I hear people talk about "the highly coveted 'Men, 18 to 34' market"—that's the phrase you always hear—I scratch my head and ask, "Why?" Why are marketers' perceptions and priorities so far out of alignment with demographic and financial reality? Clearly, PrimeTime Women ("Women, 50 and older") are the group that marketers should "covet highly."

Attitudinal Convergence: It's Biology, Silly

Overlapping all of these big external shifts that favor 50-plus women—shifts in demographics, shifts in buying power—are shifts that occur within men and women as they pass age 50. In several very suggestive ways, men's and women's attitudes converge during their mature years. The key attributes of male and female gender cultures remain in place, but the way that men and women manifest them becomes more subtle. It will behoove marketers to understand this convergence.

One key shift actually happens deep in our bodies—that is, in our hormones. Men and women engage in biochemical jujitsu, so to speak. On the one hand, men's testosterone levels drop throughout their fifties and sixties. On the other hand, women's estrogen levels drop over roughly the same time frame. Moreover, since one effect of estrogen is to suppress testosterone, 50-plus women feel the impact of testosterone far more than they did when they were younger.

Testosterone, of course, tends to promote aggressive and risk-taking behaviors. That's why, in their younger years, men are generally more assertive and more prone to seek thrills than women are. Young men, in fact, have about ten times as much testosterone as women do. But after age 50, that dynamic essentially reverses itself. (By their seventies, women have more testosterone in their blood than men do.) As a result, men and women experience testosterone in ways that make them attitudinally more alike.

Men become less aggressive, less inclined toward risk-taking, more mellow, more nurturing. That change explains why men in their fifties, after 30 years of obsessively conquering the world through their work, will suddenly look up and note with dismay that their kids have grown up and left home: "Damn, I miss my family." They are undergoing a major change in their biochemical programming.

Women, as the testosterone in their system becomes "unmasked," turn more assertive and display greater confidence. At the same time, the decrease in estrogen and other female hormones in their body causes the nurturing behaviors of their younger years to become less dominant. (Goodbye, SUV. Hello, Lexus.)

In other words—as Tom might say—PrimeTime Women totally *roar!*

Attitudinal Convergence: Intuition Is *In*

In their thought processes and in their decision making, women tend to be less linear and more intuitive than men. Similarly, 50-plus consumers rely on "wisdom" and trust their intuition—their "gut"—more than younger people do.

For women, an intuitive thinking style is hard-wired in the brain. For certain functions, the female brain has more than one processing center; not so the male brain. Women have

By their seventies, women have more testosterone in their blood than men do.

two language centers, for example. If one center gets damaged, the other center can compensate for the loss. Men have just one language center in one hemisphere. Moreover, because the connection between the left and right halves of the brain is stronger in women than in men, women are more able than men to see and integrate several pieces of information at once. As a result, women are synthesizers rather than analyzers.

For people in the 50-plus group, a preference for intuition over analysis results from the accumulation of life experience. Consider the thought process that goes into buying a car. When you're young and you haven't bought many cars in your life, all criteria seem important. You focus on gathering lots of facts and evaluating lots of features. You see the issue as a series of parts, not as a whole. But by the time you're 50 or older, you have a gut sense of which criteria really matter— matter to the use and enjoyment of a car, and matter to you personally. You're thinking is not mechanistic, but holistic and organic. It's the difference between learning a language at the level of basic grammar, and knowing a language well enough to enjoy poetry.

The implication for marketers: When trying to reach PrimeTime women (as well as her younger sisters and her 50-plus brothers), go easy on "stats and facts," and go strong on "look and feel."

Attitudinal Convergence: A Higher "Aspiration"

Men in their younger years, oriented to a hierarchical mind-set, focus on differentiating themselves from others. They respond well to aspirational marketing and appeals to envy. Women, as noted, begin with a sense that their core unit is "we" rather than "me." They believe that affiliation matters more than differentiation, and they generally care more about relating to real people than about comparing themselves with envy-inducing ideal figures.

What happens in later years, though, is that both men and women converge around a different kind of "aspiration"— around a drive to be real, to be authentic, to build a legacy on behalf of others.

Now, if you look at stages of human development, you'll see that over their life spans people of both genders move along a trajectory that maps to the male-female behavioral spectrum. There isn't a one-to-one correspondence, by any means. But the similarities—that is, the convergence on a certain outlook—are striking.

In your teens and twenties, you create your social identity. You experiment with different selves: "Am I a goth or a prep? Am I a jock or a nerd?" You worry about what other people, especially your peers, think of you: "I have to conform. I have to achieve success as the world defines success." Through your thirties and forties, you go through stages of maturation.

By the time you enter your fifties, you have a certain comfort with your social self. You've achieved a certain amount of success. And now you set your sights on expressing your *real* self. You also shift from an emphasis on worldly achievement to an emphasis on your *legacy:* "Some things that are more important than 'me.' I'll be leaving at some point. What kind of legacy will I leave behind?"

Two big marketing implications arise from this attitudinal convergence—implications that apply to women in general, to the 50-plus group, and above all to PrimeTime Women.

First, forget celebrity endorsements. These are ubiquitous. (Jack Nicklaus likes this golf club. Or Jennifer Aniston uses that hair-care product.) Yet they hold scant appeal for people in these huge market segments. For women, celebrities aren't "real"; they aren't "like you and me." For mature consumers, whose chief concern is with their "real self," celebrities are simply irrelevant.

Second, explore cause marketing, or what I call "corporate halo" marketing. Women, with their "we" orientation, really do care

trends

&

primetime women

about whether companies act like good corporate citizens. If your organization sponsors breast-cancer research, for example, play up that fact in your communications. Likewise, 50-plus consumers want to know that your company cares as much about its legacy as they care about theirs.

So build a legacy, take up a cause, don your corporate halo. If you do, PrimeTime Women, in particular, will beat a path to your door.

trends & primetime women

TOM SAYS ...

"HAT" TIP

Want to understand the PrimeTime Spirit ... truly and profoundly? Again, read Marti's next book. But while you're waiting for it, read up on the Red Hat Society. The February 2005 issue of *Executive Update* magazine has a marvelous cover story on this phenomenon—"The Red Hat Society," by Jane R. Schultz. Check it out. There's also a book by the society's founder, Sue Ellen Cooper: *The Red Hat Society: Fun and Friendship After Fifty*. And read the novel *The Red Hat Club*, by Haywood Smith, which plays on the same theme.

That theme derives from a line in the poem "Warning," by Jenny Joseph: "When I am an old woman I shall wear purple/With a red hat which doesn't go and doesn't

suit me." The Red Hat Society consists of 50-plus women who share a resolve to do whatever they want ... exuberantly ... whether it "suits" them or not. "For Cooper," writes Schultz, "the society is about harnessing the power of thoughts and feelings common to women 50 and older: camaraderie, fun, time with friends, and new friends." Beyond living according to those ideals, says Sue Ellen Cooper, "There are no rules. We want to keep it as free as possible, with no limitations. We're all tired of that."

(Dare I call them ... Red Hat Mamas?)

Businesspeople, pay heed. Hear Women Roar! Catch Maturity Mania! And learn to set your watches to the beat of ... Red-Hat-Wearing ... PrimeTime Women.

TOP 10 TO-DOs

1. *Hear them roar, hear them "boom."* Open your eyes to the convergence of two immense, underserved markets—women and Boomers. (Never has a "sweet spot" been this sweetly lucrative.)

2. *Look who's in the driver's seat.* Abandon your assumptions about "what women want." They are not all soccer moms. The new mistresses of the road: PrimeTime Women.

3. *Come to your census.* Reckon with the demographic tidal wave that is creating a huge (asset-rich) pool of 50-plus women.

4. *Do a full count.* Get over your fear of quotas, and put women on your board of directors. Fear this instead: losing touch with customers.

5. *Inherit the windfall.* Read the data on all of the wealth that Boomers will both inherit from their parents and amass for themselves. Read it, and don't weep. Instead, reap—reap that cash.

6. *Get physiological.* Take seriously the deep biological changes that women (and men, too) undergo in their mature years. As their hormones shift, so must your understanding of what motivates them.

7. *Go for the gut.* Trust PrimeTime Women (and mature men as well) to know what they want—without obsessing over "stats and facts."

8. *Toss those testimonials.* Close up that checkbook that you use to buy celebrity endorsements. PrimeTime Women aspire to be their best—not to be someone else.

9. *Wear your corporate halo.* Practice and promote good works by your company. PrimeTime Women spend time—and, yes, money—on their legacy. They expect you to do the same.

10. *Leave your red hat on.* Help PrimeTime Women exult in the freedom to wear a big red hat if they so desire. (Don't forget: They can afford any hat they want.)

INDEX

AUTHOR'S ACKNOWLEDGMENTS

It required a far-flung virtual village to make this book. Here I wish to note a few "essential" residents of that village: Michael Slind, editor, and Jason Godfrey, designer, both continued the sterling work that helped make my previous book (*Re-imagine!*) so sharply compelling. In adapting that book to make this one, they both achieved the noble feat of reinventing the project from within. Stephanie Jackson, of Dorling Kindersley, pushed and pushed—and charmed and charmed—this book into being. Also at DK, Peter Luff used his sense of visual panache to help produce a "small" book with big impact, and Dawn Henderson applied her editorial talent deftly, creatively, and crucially at every stage of the project. Erik Hansen served in his usual role of "project manager," though that term fails to capture the unique mix of doggedness and nimbleness that he brings to all of my publishing ventures. Cathy Mosca attended to details of authorial execution and factual accuracy with her typical vigilance. My thanks to them all.

PERMISSIONS

Grateful acknowledgment is made to the following: The Associated Press: Excerpts from "Forever Young" by Colleen Long. Reprinted with permission; The Economist: Exerpts from "Over 60 and Overlooked" © The Economist Newspapers Ltd, London, 10 August 2002; The New York Times Co.: Excerpts from "One Woman's Account of Two Hotel Experiences," by Joe Sharkey © 2002 by the New York Times Co. Reprinted with permission.

PICTURE CREDITS

Picture Researcher : Sarah Hopper
DK Picture Library : Richard Dabb

The publisher would like to thank the following for their kind permission to reproduce their photographs;
(Abbreviations key; t=top, b=below, r=right, l=left, c=centre, a=above, tl=top left, tr=top right, bl=below left, br=below right).

10: Corbis/Mark L.Stephenson; 14: Corbis/Alan Schein Photography; 19: Kobal Collection/Universal; 21: Corbis/Ronnie Kaufman (t), Corbis/Walter Smith (b); 26: Corbis/Ted Horowitz; 27: Getty Images/Tom Schierlitz; 29: Corbis/Jose Luis Pelaez, Inc.; 32: Corbis/Charles Gupton; 33: Getty Images/Clarissa Leahy; 36-37: Getty Images/James Muldowney; 40: Getty Images/Wally McNamee; 52: Corbis/Anton Daix (r), Corbis/Norma Zuniga (l); 57: Corbis/Brian A.Vikander (t), Corbis/Sam Sharpe (b); 58: Corbis/Ondrea Barbe (tl), Corbis/Randy Faris (tr); 59: Corbis/Dennis Wilson (tl), Corbis/Michael Prince (tr); 60: Corbis/Pete Stone (b), Corbis/Randy Faris (t); 65: Corbis/Coneyl Jay; 66: Corbis/David Katzenstein (b), Corbis/Franco Vogt (t); 68-69: Corbis/L.Clarke; 75: Corbis/Eric Curry (b), Corbis/T.R.Tharp (t); 85: Corbis/Ronnie Kaufman; 87: Corbis/Tom Stewart; 88: Corbis/Jose Luis Pelaez Inc. (tr), Corbis/Strauss/Curtis (tl); 89: Corbis/John Henley (tr), Corbis/ Jose Luis Pelaez Inc.(tcr); 90: Corbis/M.L.Sinibaldi (b), Corbis/Paul Anthony (t); 93: Corbis/Edward Bock (b), Corbis/Maiman Rick (t); 94-95: Corbis/Phil Banko; 96: dutchboy.com; 99: Corbis/Didier Robcis; 100: Corbis/Laureen March; 102-103: Corbis/Roy McMahon; 105: Corbis/Najlah Feanny; 113: Corbis/Jim Naughten; 119: Corbis/Gabe Palmer (t), Corbis/George Shelley (b); 122: Getty Images/Donna Day (b); 122-123: Corbis/Robert Daly (b), Magnum/David Hurn (t); 123: Getty Images/Thomas Hoeffgen (t); 124: Corbis/Rob Lewine (b), Science Photo Library/Scott Camazine (t); 126: Corbis/Cooperphoto (t), Corbis/Randy Faris (b); 128: Retna Pictures Ltd/Armando Gallo; 129: NTT Do Co Mo Inc.; 143: Corbis/Chuck Savage (b), Corbis/Dex Images (t); 144: Corbis/George Shelley (l), Zefa Visual Media/C.Lyttle (r); 145: Corbis/Darren Modricker (r), Zefa Visual Media/D.Ramazani (l); 148: Zefa Visual Media/O.Graf (r); 151: Corbis/Douglas Peebles (b), Corbis/Tim McGuire (t); 153: Corbis/Tony Roberts.

All other images © Dorling Kindersley.
For further information see:
www.dkimages.com

Hear Tom Peters Live with Red Audio (TM).

FOR THE CURIOUS ...
Source notes on the stories and data cited in this book are available online (www.tompeters.com/essentials/notes.php). For complete versions of the Cool Friends interviews (www.tompeters.com/cool_friends/friends.php).

ABOUT THE AUTHORS

TOM PETERS   *The Economist called Tom Peters the Uber-guru. BusinessWeek labelled him "business's best friend and worst nightmare." Fortune tagged him as the Ur-guru of management, and compared him to Ralph Waldo Emerson, Henry David Thoreau, Walt Whitman, and H.L. Mencken. In an in-depth study released by Accenture's Institute for Strategic Change in 2002, he scored second among the top 50 "Business Intellectuals," behind Michael Porter and ahead of Peter Drucker.*

Tom's first book, coauthored with Robert J. Waterman, was In Search of Excellence (1982). National Public Radio in 1999 placed the book among the "Top Three Business Books of the Century," and a poll by Bloomsbury Publishing in 2002 ranked it as the "greatest business book of all time." Tom followed Search with a string of international best-sellers: A Passion for Excellence (1985, with Nancy Austin), Thriving on Chaos (1987), Liberation Management (1992), The Tom Peters Seminar: Crazy Times Call for Crazy Organizations (1993), The Pursuit of WOW! (1994); The Circle of Innovation: You Can't Shrink Your Way to Greatness (1997), and a series of books on Reinventing Work—The Brand You50, The Project50, and The Professional Service Firm50 (1999). In 2003 Tom joined with publisher Dorling Kindersley to release Re-imagine! Business Excellence in a Disruptive Age. That book, which aims to reinvent the business book through energetic presentation of critical ideas, immediately became an international No.1 bestseller.

Born in Baltimore in 1942, Tom resided in Northern California from 1974 to 2000 and now lives on a 1,600-acre working farm in Vermont with his wife, Susan Sargent. He has degrees in civil engineering from Cornell University (B.C.E., M.C.E.) and in business from Stanford University (M.B.A., Ph.D.). He holds honorary doctorates from several institutions, including the State University of Management in Moscow (2004). Serving in the U.S. Navy from 1966 to 1970, he made two deployments to Vietnam (as a Navy Seabee) and survived a tour in the Pentagon. He also served as a senior White House drug-abuse advisor from 1973 to 1974. From 1974 to 1981, he worked at McKinsey & Co., becoming a partner and Organization Effectiveness practice leader in 1979. Tom is a Fellow of the International Academy of Management, the World Productivity Association, the International Customer Service Association, and the Society for Quality and Participation. Today, he presents about 75 major seminars each year (half of them outside the United States), and participates in numerous other learning events, both in person and on the Web.

MARTHA BARLETTA   *The president and CEO of the TrendSight Group, Marti is a recognized authority on gender-focused marketing strategies and helps companies boost sales by tapping into the buying power of women. She is also the author of Marketing to Women: How to Understand, Reach, and Increase Your Share of the World's Largest Market Segment. The book, now in its sixth printing, is available in 13 languages (including Japanese, Chinese, and Russian); a second edition will be published in 2005. Her next book, whose working title is "PrimeTime Women: The Marketing Bull's-Eye," is scheduled to appear in 2006.*

Marti possesses a command of her subject and a passionate, lively style that have made her a popular speaker at conferences, business schools, and corporate events. She has been quoted on CBS Evening News, NBC Nightly News, CNN, and First Business TV, as well as in the Wall Street Journal, Fast Company, BusinessWeek, Brandweek, Entrepreneur, Advertising Age, AdGenius, Adnews (Australia), Dagens Industri (Sweden), Diario Economico (Portugal), and many other publications worldwide. Marti, a Wharton M.B.A., honed her marketing and sales talents through her work at such top-flight agencies as McCann-Erickson, TLK, FCB, and Frankel, and on blue-chip brands such as Kraft, Kodak, and Wachovia.

SAY IT LOUD – THE ESSENTIALS MANIFESTO

They say...   I say...

They say...	I say...
Sure, we need "change."	We need REVOLUTION. NOW.
Your (my) language is extreme.	The times are extreme.
I am extreme.	I am a realist.
I demand too much.	"They" accept mediocrity too readily.
Brand You is not for everyone.	The alternative is unemployment.
Take a deep breath. Be calm.	Tell it to Wal*Mart. Tell it to China. Tell it to India. Tell it to Dell. Tell it to Microsoft.
What's wrong with a "good product"?	Wal*Mart or China or both are about to eat your lunch. Why can't you provide instead a Fabulous Experience?
The Web is a "useful tool."	The Web changes everything. Now.
We need an "initiative."	We need a Dream. And Dreamers.
Great Design is nice.	Great Design is mandatory.
You (I) overplay the "women's thing."	The minuscule share of Women in Senior Leadership Positions is a Waste and a Disgrace and a Strategic Marketing Error.
We need a "project" to explore "new markets."	We need Total Strategic Realignment to exploit the Women and Boomer markets.
"Wow" is "typical Tom."	"WOW" is a Minimum Survival Requirement.
We like people who, with steely determination, say, "I can make it better."	I love people who, with a certain maniacal gleam in their eye, perhaps even a giggle, say, "I can turn the world upside-down!"
Let's speed things up.	Let's transform the Corporate Metabolism until Insane Urgency becomes a Sacrament.
We want recruits with "spotless records."	Those "spots" are what defines Talent.
We favor a "team" that works in "harmony."	Give me a raucous brawl among the most creative people imaginable.
We want "happy" customers.	Give me pushy, needy, nasty, provocative customers who will drag me down Innovation Boulevard at 100mph.
We want to partner with "best of breed."	Give me Coolest of Breed.
Happy balance.	Creative Tension.
Peace, brother.	Bruise my feelings. Flatten my ego. SAVE MY JOB.
Plan it.	DO IT.
Market share.	Market Creation.
Basic black.	TECHNICOLOR RULES!
Conglomerate and Imitate.	Create and Innovate.
Improve and Maintain.	DESTROY and RE-IMAGINE!